Inventive Assemblies for Inclusive Schools

Margaret and Dennis Goldthorpe

Acknowledgements

Just saying 'Thank you' to people who have helped us to write a book seems inadequate. Perhaps it would be better if we threw a party. If we did, it would be a very lively party as there are so many people to thank.

First, we should like to thank all of the children at Alexandra School. They are true assembly stars. They will always join in with enormous gusto, they cheer each other and the staff to the rafters, they laugh like drains at assembly jokes, and you can always be sure of a forest of hands up when you ask them questions. (Although in retrospect, perhaps Dennis did go a bit far with that rabbit!)

We should like to thank all of the staff at Alexandra School for their help and ideas, but especially Perdy Buchanan-Barrow and Charlie Hayward. They gave encouragement and real help (and tea and chocolate cake) at an especially 'stuck' moment.

We should also like to thank Linda Renfrew, headteacher of Hoe Bridge Pre-Preparatory School, Woking, for trialling our assemblies. She is a terrific headteacher and the Independent Association of Prep Schools are lucky to have her example.

We should like to thank our children for, yet again, enduring the domestic stress and mess that writing books always engenders.

But if this were a party, Corin Redsell – our kind, clever, patient editor – would be guest of honour. Thank you so much, Corin, for all your hard work and encouragement.

Sarratt Bottom, Hertfordshire, 2009

The rights of Margaret Goldthorpe and Dennis Goldthorpe to be identified as the authors of this work have been asserted by them in accordance with sections 77 and 78 of the Copyright, Designs and Patents Act 1988.

Inventive Assemblies for Inclusive Schools
106521
ISBN-13: 978 1 85503 484 6
© Margaret Goldthorpe and Dennis Goldthorpe
All rights reserved
Illustrations © Garry Davies
First published 2009. Reprinted 2010
Printed in the UK for LDA
LDA, Findel Education, Hyde Buildings, Ashton Road, Cheshire, SK14 4SH

Contents

Introduction

Schools, like nations, have to manage the delicate balance of celebrating wide cultural and religious diversity whilst simultaneously creating a strong allegiance to the team, whether that team is the country or the school.

There are those who believe that the only way to do this is to adopt a particular culture or faith, decide that will be the norm, and attempt to ally each child and adult to that culture or faith tradition. There are others who try to eradicate all evidence of faiths or cultures within a school.

Our preference and belief is that we should accommodate all faiths and cultures and celebrate them equally.

There is, however, a considerable consequent difficulty if you adopt this option. How do you build your team? On what is it founded? How do you generate a true sense of belonging to 'Team: Our School?' What is it going to be that gives us the immense sense of belonging that is needed for us to be able to overcome our selfish wants and desires and put the good of our team first?

Our solution has always been to have a set of school values that are clear, unambiguous and inclusive. It is on these values that the school is built. Children and adults alike subscribe to these values. They are our guiding principles and the banner behind which we are all happy to walk. They are what make us a team.

The set of values we recommend is this:

- **treat others as you would like to be treated**
- **forgive**
- **share**
- **listen**

- be honest and live with integrity
- be kind and helpful
- do your best to be your best self.

Having a set of values is one thing. Living out these values is quite another. How do we help children to do this?

As well as praising children for their success in living by these values and using appropriate sanctions if they choose to ignore them, we believe discussion and reflection on these values is important.

Assembly is a wonderful opportunity to say to your school:

> OK, everyone, this is us. All of us. Adults and children together. What do we believe is right? What does our school have to say about all the difficult situations we are likely to meet in school and in our lives in the wider world? How are we, collectively, going to handle difficult situations? What is our inclusive creed? What governs the choices we make every day, choices that impact upon the happiness and well-being of ourselves and others?

> People will know us as a school, as a team, by the way we behave. How do we want people to judge Team: Our School?

> And, perhaps most importantly, what benefits are there for each of us when we live supported and loved by our team? When you belong to Team: Our School, you should never feel an outsider, excluded or alone.

These assemblies are designed to promote discussion and encourage ideas. More than anything, we want children to be able to look at each other and think:

> You may dress differently from me, speak differently from me, worship differently or not at all, but you are my friend. You are part of my team and I want the very best for you, every day you are in this school and throughout your whole life.

The proof
of the pudding

A good assembly for September when there are new parents present.

Theme

This assembly works well at the beginning of the year. Invite the Reception children's parents along for a 'Show and Tell' assembly. This is an excellent time to put across the message that we value parents, that they are part of the school and that we are all working together. Parents need to feel loved and valued by the school. It's always good to get them on our side from the beginning.

Preparation

You are going to present two summer puddings: one you will make the day before the assembly (so you have the vital prop when you say 'Here is one I made earlier') and one you will construct in front of the parents and children. Therefore you will need to do some fairly serious preparation for this assembly. Sorry, but it is worth it. We have done it a couple of times and it doesn't fail you.

You will need the ingredients and equipment for two summer puddings:

- ✪ Two large white loaves, not sliced. It's fine if the bread is a bit stale.
- ✪ Two 500g (1 lb) bags or boxes of frozen summer fruits. You must have red fruits – strawberries, raspberries, cherries, blackberries, blueberries, redcurrants, blackcurrants, and so on. Do not, under any circumstances, get tropical fruits such as melon and mango mixtures.
- ✪ 160 g (6 oz) caster sugar.
- ✪ A saucepan for simmering the fruit.
- ✪ A third bowl to store the pre-cooked fruit in for the assembly the next day.
- ✪ You will need two 500 ml (1 pint) glass pudding basins. It is important that they are glass; this is a visual assembly.

✪ Two saucers that will fit just inside the top of the bowls.

✪ A demonstration table.

✪ Weights – you can use bags of rice, jars of jam, tins of beans, or anything else that comes to hand.

✪ A knife for running round the edge of the pudding and a plate for turning it out.

The day before the assembly make the first summer pudding completely, and half make the second.

This assembly is easier to do than to explain, we promise you.

1 Put nearly all of the fruit in a pan, saving a few of each frozen fruit for the demonstration tomorrow.

2 Pour all the sugar over the fruit and stir gently to mix.

3 Add 2 tablespoons of water.

4 Place the pan over moderate heat and bring gently to the boil. When the juices are beginning to flow, raise the heat slightly and simmer for about 2–3 minutes.

5 While the fruit is simmering, cut the bread into slices and remove all the crusts.

6 Completely line both glass pudding basins with bread, including the bottom of the basins. You may need to overlap the slices slightly and press them together. You don't want any gaps.

7 Divide the fruit mixture into two. Pour one half into a bowl for tomorrow and pour the other half into one of the bread-lined basins. The juice should seep into the bread overnight and turn the bread red. To be certain, you may want to soak the bread slices in the juice before lining the bowl. We know it's cheating – but you don't want a failed pudding.

8 Make a lid with a slice of bread and put it over the fruit. Your summer pudding is now enclosed by bread. Cover with the saucer and put the weight(s) on top.

9 Refrigerate.

In the morning don't forget to remove the pudding from the fridge and take it to school with all the other bits and pieces you need.

The assembly

The assembly itself is quite short. This is to allow time for the children's Show and Tell.

Have your demonstration table ready. Keep your ready-made summer pudding under a cloth – you need a 'Ta Da!' moment!

Good morning, everyone. I am so pleased to be able to welcome you to our school. As you know, we are very proud of our school. It has *[name a few key features – library area, resources room, outdoor classroom, new or newly decorated classroom, splendid PE hall, great stage, adventure playground – all the parts of the building that you are proud of]* and we are really proud of these.

We are all very good at keeping our school building looking its best. We don't drop litter, our caretaker keeps everywhere smart, we regularly paint and we look after the garden.

But a school building is just a building. It needs something else to become a real school.

Now, last night I was thinking of making a summer pudding for myself, and that made me think about our school. Can you see this bowl? It's lined with bread, because that's how you start to make a summer pudding. After that you put in the fruit.

I started thinking that the bread casing is like the school building. It's very important and it matters that it is properly made. Look at how all the bread joins up so the pudding won't break when I turn it out.

And here we have the fruit. *[Show them the fruit you kept back from the cooking.]* This fruit is like all of the adults and children associated with the school. We have strawberries and raspberries and blackcurrants and cherries, all wonderful, but all separate. In life we have children and teachers and learning assistants and mums and dads and cooks and clerical staff. Outside school everyone is separate and each of us is different.

But what happens when we all come together? How do we make a school?

Well, first we mix all the people together, just as all this fruit was cooked together. *[Show them the bowl of cooked fruit.]* And do you know what brought out the juice in the fruit? Sugar. We mixed in sugar and that made it juicy.

In school we mix in love, which brings everyone together.

Then we put all the fruit into the bread-lined bowl, just as we put everyone into the school. *[Pour the summer fruits into the basin.]* Now we put the roof on. *[Add the bread lid.]*

But this pudding is not finished. To make a summer pudding you need a little time. And it's the same with school. At the beginning of the year we have new children, new parents and new staff and maybe people don't know each other.

But after a couple of weeks this is what happens. *[Take the cloth off the pre-cooked summer pudding. This is your 'Ta Da!' moment!]* The school is changed, like this pudding. Look how the pudding is all pink. The fruit inside has mixed together and the dull white bread is now pink and juicy and sweet, as our school is after a couple of weeks. It's not a dead space with lots of strangers in it any more. It's completely changed. All the people have mixed in with each other, everyone has got to know everyone else, and the school is influenced by all of the adults and children who belong here.

Look at the bread. It's delicious and completely soaked in fruit. The whole pudding is one scrumptious whole. And that's what we want our school to be like, with the staff, the parents and the children all getting along together and making our school one delicious whole.

Now let's see if we can turn it out. *[Gently run the knife round the rim of the bowl. Put the plate on the top and turn the pudding over. It should slide out.]*

After assembly I am going to give each of the parents a taste of this summer pudding. Just a spoonful on a saucer. It will taste wonderful and remind us that separately we can be fine, but together we can make something really, really special.

Prayer

Dear Lord, help us to be the sweetness that makes the juice to bring us all together.

Thought for the day

Separately we can be fine, but together we can become something really, really special.

A bit of a yarn

Theme

We all have different skills and talents – but we all need each other to get the best from those skills and talents.

Preparation

You will need two knitting needles, a ball of wool and a knitting pattern. Any needles, any wool (although the more colourful, the better) and any pattern. You may have all of this in school or at home. If not, do not worry. Many charity shops have masses of knitting equipment and only charge small amounts for it.

You will also need a chair to sit on. If you have an armchair in school somewhere and can get it on to the stage, then so much the better – but that is just set dressing.

The assembly

As the children come in, they find you sitting at the front of the hall or on the stage. You are on the chair or in the armchair. You are knitting. If you can't knit at all, ask someone on the staff who can to cast on and knit a couple of rows for you. Then you can pretend to knit. You never know, your knitting pal might teach you how to do it yourself. When the children are all seated you continue to knit if you can, or put the knitting in your lap if you can't, and begin to speak to the school.

Below is a script – but you won't need to read it. You will be able to chat to the children. It's not a complicated plot.

> Good morning, school. You know, I had a dreadfully annoying evening last night. I sat down to watch the television and do a bit of knitting. I want

to finish these gloves / this scarf / this jumper [whatever] by winter / for Christmas / for my sister's birthday and it's going to take a long time.

Well, everything was fine for a while, then I got up to make a cup of tea. When I got back I could not find one of the needles. I looked and looked. 'Well,' I thought, 'I can't knit with just one needle – I'll have to stop.'

But then I found it down the side of the cushion. That was a relief. I was able to carry on.

But two minutes later I realised I needed to look at the pattern and I couldn't find my glasses. I tried to make the pattern up as I went along but it was hopeless. I just don't have enough knitting skills to make up patterns. I thought I would have to stop again.

Then I realised my glasses were on my head, so I read the pattern and carried on. Next I ran out of wool. Now that was a disaster. No wool, no knitting!

However, I had a look in the knitting bag and found another ball, so I was able to carry on again.

The next problem came a few moments later, when I tried to follow a difficult part of the pattern and could not understand it.

I went next door to my neighbour, who is very good at knitting, and she explained it all to me. I came home and carried on happily knitting. Then another really big disaster happened.

The cat jumped on to my lap and started to play with the wool. Oh, the mess! Everything was getting tangled up. I was so cross. In the end I had to put her out into the garden as she was spoiling all of my hard work.

Now, all of those problems got me thinking about school.

You see, our school is a bit like this knitting. We need all of us to make it work.

I needed two needles, beautiful wool, a pattern, my glasses and a clever friend to help me. If any of these had been missing, I would have been stuck.

In our school it's the same.

We need practical people who are like the needles.

We need artistic people who are like the beautiful wool.

We need technical and mathematical people who are like the pattern.

We need a bit of help if we have special needs. Our helpers are like the glasses.

And we need helpful teachers to explain how to do the difficult things in school. They are like my friend next door.

We all need each other. We might think we can manage without someone and their skills, but we really can't.

Oh, except that cat. What I didn't need was a cat that decided to be naughty and tried to tangle everything up. We really don't need anyone to be like that cat.

Prayer

Dear God, you have not made us to live alone. You have told us that we all belong to each other and we are all important to each other. Just as our bodies need their different parts, so our school needs the different people. Help us to care for each other, valuing everyone's differing skills and everyone's contribution to our school.

Thought for the day

Let us never think that our skills are superior to those of others. We need each other's talents if we are to make something beautiful of our world.

Batteries
not included

Theme

This assembly arose after a little boy who was being told off for some minor misdemeanour in the dining hall said that it was not his fault he was being naughty – it was because he had special needs. As the misdemeanour had nothing to do with his particular learning problems, it seemed that an assembly on the topic of free choice was necessary.

Preparation

This needs a bit of preparation as you have to locate a few particular toys.

You will need:

- ✪ A couple of remote-controlled cars plus the controller.
- ✪ A battery-operated dog or cat (you know, the kind that mindlessly trundles about, occasionally turning somersaults, but is somehow rather cute).
- ✪ Any other robotic toys that you can locate.
- ✪ If you know someone who has one, a robotic vacuum cleaner would be amazing. (We have never met either a robotic cleaner or an owner!)
- ✪ Make sure you have plenty of batteries for all of these toys.

The assembly

Get all the toys going before you start the assembly. You want the children to be transfixed by all of this wondrous activity as they arrive. Have on hand an assistant who can help you keep the robots under control and can turn them off when it's time.

Good morning, everyone. Do you like all of these robotic toys? They are wonderful, aren't they!

I like them enormously. Look, I can control this car. *[Practise a bit first so that you know you can.]* It does exactly what I want it to do. Look, I want it to go forward and it does; I want it to go left and it does. Marvellous.

Spend a couple of minutes showing the children how fantastic all the toys are, emphasising that they are under your control – they have no will of their own. If the dog gives you any trouble, stick it against a wall, where it will do endless somersaults.

I've got you all here today to tell you that I have decided to send you home forever and just keep these wonderful robots. *[Now turn them off.]*

You see, yesterday a little boy told me that it was not his fault he was being silly in the lunch queue. He said he could not help it.

That got me thinking about all the other times people tell me that their behaviour is not their fault. I realised that children are always telling me that other people made them do things: 'He made me kick him', 'She made me lose my temper', 'I couldn't help swearing.'

So I thought to myself, 'Well, all of these children seem to think they have no control over their behaviour. They seem to think they are robots. Robots are controlled by forces outside themselves, and they have no free will.'

I thought some more about that. If they are robots, why am I bothering with all the effort of running a school?

I am not going to bother any more. I am sending you home and I am going to get in some electronic robots instead. It will be brilliant!

Whenever they are too noisy, I will turn them off.

I will sack all of the kitchen staff because robots don't need food – I just have to buy a big box of rechargeable batteries.

I will sell the playground to a supermarket because robots don't need to play.

I will sell the playing field because robots don't need exercise.

I will sack the teachers. I will install USB ports in all the robots. Then, instead of tiring lessons, I'll download everything that I want them to know, load it on to a pen drive and plug the pen drive into the USB ports.

This is marvellous. If any of the robots go wrong, I'll get the engineers in or break them up for scrap.

No more troublesome children!

Of course, you children won't mind because some of you think you are robots anyway. Certainly that little boy did yesterday.

Shall I do all of that? *[Take answers.]*

Who thinks there is no difference between a child and a robot?

Who thinks there is a difference?

Well, that's quite a few.

Well, I agree with you. I think children are better than robots. I like children, You make me laugh, you tell me stories about home, you write wonderful stories, and you teach me brilliant games. So don't go telling me you are a robot, any of you. Don't say you can't help doing things.

What's the difference between a boy or girl and a robot?

Take a few answers. Be prepared to parry the ludicrous ideas.

You are right. The big difference is that a boy or girl can think. A boy or girl can choose how they behave.

So what can you do to stop yourself from getting into trouble? You can't just find a button that says TROUBLE and turn it off.

No, you have to locate your brain and turn it to THINK and to CHOOSE.

THINK – What is the right thing to do? What would be the stupid thing to do? Shall I do the stupid thing (which might be fun but is wrong) or the sensible thing?

CHOOSE – I choose the sensible thing.

Who can tell me about a time when they had to make a choice about how to behave? *[Take a few examples.]*

Now you know you are not a robot. You choose how to behave.

Right – let's put these robots away. I don't really want a school full of robots; they don't know any good jokes.

And anyway – I'd miss you lot far too much.

Prayer

Lord, you made us all to be unique. You also gave us the power to choose our actions. Give us wisdom to understand the choices and courage when the choices are hard.

Thought for the day

We create ourselves through the choices we make.

Don't just stand there, do something

Theme

This assembly is rather a good pre-Christmas assembly, if for no other reason than that it needs all the curtains or blinds to be closed and the room lit by fairy lights. You can get the lights up for Christmas and then use them for this assembly. The aim is to remind children that if they do nothing good, nothing good happens.

Preparation

At the start of this assembly the blinds or curtains should be drawn and the ordinary lights should be on. Have a person standing by to switch off the main lights and switch on the fairy lights.

You will need a table in front of you with the following items laid out on it:

- ✪ child's sock
- ✪ pen and writing paper
- ✪ bucket and sponge for car washing
- ✪ mobile phone
- ✪ exercise book
- ✪ gardening trowel
- ✪ box of matches
- ✪ large pillar candle.

The assembly

Good morning, everyone. It's nearly Christmas, isn't it?

I was going to make a Christmas cake this year, but I didn't get round to it.

I was also going to make my Christmas pudding this year – but I didn't get round to that either.

And I thought I might make my Christmas cards, but it's too late for that now too.

I often find this happens. I know what I should do. I know what I want to do. But somehow I just don't do it.

Does that ever happen to you?

Do you ever know what you should do but don't do it, and then feel awful?

Here are some examples:

O *[Pick up the sock.]* Who has ever thought 'I ought to tidy my bedroom', but has not got round to it?

O *[Pick up the pen and paper.]* Who has ever thought 'I ought to write my thank-you letters' after a birthday or Christmas but ended up only writing one, to their grandma?

O *[Pick up the bucket and sponge.]* Who has ever decided to be really helpful and clean their mum's or dad's car, but it never seems to be quite the right day for it?

O *[Pick up the mobile phone.]* Who has ever thought 'I must ring up my friend who left school last year and see how they are getting on in their new school', and never got round to ringing?

O *[Pick up the exercise book.]* Who has ever thought they ought to get on with their homework, but just carried on playing with their PlayStation or chatting on MSN?

O *[Pick up the trowel.]* How many teachers have ever thought 'I must weed the garden' but not got round to it?

You see, we know what we ought to do, but sometimes laziness affects us and we don't do the right thing.

The trouble is, if we do nothing good, nothing good happens. In fact, if we do nothing good, bad things often happen.

The room won't tidy itself, the car won't wash itself and the letters won't write themselves.

What will happen is that your room will get more and more messy and more and more horrible to be in. Your friends and relations will get increasingly fed up with you for not writing thank-you letters and they will stop sending you presents. Your mum and dad will get cross and disappointed and the car will get dirtier. Your friend will forget you.

Your homework will back up and you will get into masses of trouble at school.

The garden will turn into a wilderness.

A famous Irish writer called Edmund Burke once said:

> *All that is necessary for the triumph of evil is that good men do nothing.*

That means if the good people do nothing, the bad people win.

What should we do if our friends start being unkind about someone behind their back?

We should say something. Perhaps 'Don't let's gossip. It makes me feel awful.'

What should we do if we hear someone make a racist remark?

We should say something. Perhaps, 'I don't think it's right to make racist remarks. I don't think we should do it.'

What if we see someone laugh at someone who has trouble walking?

We should say 'Please don't let's laugh at Susan *[or whoever]*, it's hard enough for her without us making things worse.'

But these are things we have to be bothered to do.

It's like the things on this table. If we don't do the good thing, the bad thing will happen.

There is wrong and there is right.

Every time we do nothing and let something wrong win, the world gets a little darker.

Every time we stand up for what is right, we are a light in that darkness and the world gets a little brighter.

If we let a lot of bad things or bad people win, the world ends up like this. *[This is the signal for the main lights to go off. The room is now in darkness.]*

Every time we stand up for what is right we are like a little light in the darkness. *[Light the candle on the table.]*

But if we all stand up for what is right, the world looks more like this. *[This is the signal for the fairy lights to go on. The room is now lit by your candle and hundreds of twinkly lights.]*

Each one of these lights is someone standing up for what is right. Do you want to shine?

Then be brave and fight the darkness.

Now we are going to listen to a song and think about how we are going to shine. *[Go to* http://www.youtube.com/watch?v=G7WyCK-HmVs; *with thanks to Matt Redman.]*

Prayer

Lord, help us to shine like stars in the universe, holding out God's truth in the darkest place. Help us to live for your glory.

Thought for the day

'All that is necessary for the triumph of evil is that good men do nothing' – Edmund Burke (1729–1797), Irish orator, philosopher and politician.

Everyone is good at something

Theme

This assembly is very visual and should be fairly well understood by children who find wordy assemblies fly over their heads.

The assembly speaks for itself. We are all good at something and our job as teachers is to spot the talent in every child and nurture it.

Preparation

This assembly is a little complicated and requires some preparation. However, it is fun because it's one of those assemblies in which all the teachers are seen to misbehave – always a winner!

There are eight 'children', who are played by teachers.

We suggest you photocopy this assembly and give a copy to each of the teachers taking part. It would be a good idea to have a short rehearsal.

Ask the teachers taking part to get their own props and give them to you the day before the assembly or at the rehearsal. This is not difficult for them to do, and it will mean you aren't running about all week looking for bits and pieces, and you don't have to put the whole lot away or give them all back after you've done. Delegation is a good way forward.

You will need to hand each of the 'children' their props during the assembly, so have them all ready, near at hand.

The props are as follows:

Child 1: song book.

Child 2: bat and ball of some description, perhaps a cricket bat or tennis racquet or hockey stick and ball.

Child 3: item of percussion (cymbals or drum).

Child 4: pair of trainers.

Child 5: play script.

Child 6: football.

Child 7: pair of gardening gloves.

Child 8: pencils and sketchbook.

You will need enough desks or tables for the 'children'. These tables should be placed sideways on to the main body of the hall, in the manner of a classroom. You will not need a table.

You may want to change this assembly to suit the clubs and activities you have in your school. Alternatively this assembly may inspire you to start a couple of new clubs.

The assembly

The stage or front of hall is set up like a classroom. There are seven 'children' sitting at the tables. The eighth one is going to run in late. These are the pupils. You stand up and address them.

Good morning, children.

You then say that you are going to take the register. Call out the first name. We suggest you use names that are typical of your school but not recognisable as actual children. You do not want children to think you are laughing at them – if they do, they will be justifiably angry. You do need the type of names that will mean the children enjoy a bit of recognition humour, so choose names that are appropriate.

As soon as you start to call the register, the 'children' start to misbehave. As well as general calling out and fooling around, they also do the following:

Child 1: answers the register in a silly sing-song voice.

Child 2: rolls up bits of paper into balls and, using a ruler, flicks them at other children. They try not to miss their mark.

Child 3: starts drumming on their table.

Child 4: comes running in late.

Child 5: shouts out (clean) limericks.

Child 6: produces a ball and starts dribbling it around the classroom.

Child 7: stares out of an imaginary window.

Child 8: scribbles on their table.

Throughout all of this you are telling them off and trying, fruitlessly, to restore order. Let everything get really out of hand. Then take control.

Stop! *[They stop and become quiet.]*

This is madness. I have a class full of talented children and all of their talents are going to waste.

[Call out child 1.] When I ask you to say your name for the register, I don't expect you to sing out in a manner designed to annoy. You have got a good voice. Don't waste it. Join the choir. Come to choir every Monday lunchtime. I bet you will have a solo ready to sing by the time of the summer concert if you work hard. *[Give them the song book and send them back to their seat. They look through the book with interest.]*

[Call out child 2.] Why aren't you in the cricket team? You hit every one of those paper balls. That takes really good hand–eye co-ordination. Stop wasting your time messing about in class and be sure to see *[name PE teacher]* at lunchtime. Here, take this. *[Give them the bat and ball.]* You might play for *[name county]* one day if you work really hard.

[Call out child 3.] Your drumming on the desk is going to drive me mad! Drumming is difficult and you seem to be very good at it, though. Go along to *[name the music teacher]* this week and ask about learning to play percussion. That means the drums, the triangle, the cymbals and even the bells. We need all the talented musicians we can get. You will have to work at it, but you seem to like practising. Here, take this *[hand the child the instrument you have]* and start to practise at lunchtime.

[Call out child 4.] Why do you run everywhere? No, don't answer that. Just make sure you are at the sports day practice this lunchtime. If you keep running like that you can get into the athletics team. Of course, you will

have to learn to turn up to practices and never be late. But if you work very hard you could be a good runner. Take these. *[Hand them the trainers.]*

[Call out child 5.] Shouting out limericks in class is not acceptable. However, performing in the school play is most welcome. Take this script *[hand them the script]* and make sure you go to the read-through for the summer term play on Wednesday. You are obviously a born performer and I don't want such talent to go to waste.

[Call out child 6, who brings the football with them.] Are you already in the football team?

Child: Yes, Miss/Sir.

You: Well done! But save the practising for the field, please!

[Call out child 7.] You have been staring out of the window since you sat down. Do you wish you were outside?

Child: Yes. I don't like being indoors.

You: Right. Then you had better join the gardening club. Take these gloves. The gardeners meet by the front door on Tuesdays and Thursdays. They are planting *[something seasonal]* at the moment. They would be pleased to have you. Do you mind being cold and wet?

Child: No.

You: You will make a good gardener.

[Call out child 8.] Drawing on the desk is dreadful behaviour. Drawing in a sketchbook is excellent behaviour. Take this sketchbook, fill it up and come back to me for a new one, and never ever let me catch you drawing on a table again.

[Face the school.] Now, these children all looked like naughty children when I was taking the register, didn't they? What they were doing wasn't naughty. They were simply doing it at an inappropriate time.

In fact, they all showed great talents and skills – skills and talents some of them didn't even know they had.

At this school we know that every single one of you is good at one thing at least, and many of you are good at several things.

Someone once said that the secret of a happy life is to find out what you like to do – and then make a career out of it. We try to help you find your talents, and then give you somewhere to practise them. Your job is to work hard with the talents that you have been given so that you can be the best person you can be. Make sure that you practise in the right place, not the wrong one.

Now I want each of you to go away. Through the week notice what you like doing. Then we can talk to you about how you can pursue that in school.

Prayer

Dear God, help us to be careful with the gifts and talents you have given us. Let us not waste them, but use them and develop them.

Thought for the day

Our talents are like precious seeds – they need nurture, not neglect.

Lessons from fishing

Theme

When children are made upset by other children, one of the pieces of advice often given to them is 'Stay away from those children if they are upsetting you.' This is often hopeless advice. We cannot stay away from people we are with all day in the close confines of a classroom, dining hall, playground or sports field.

This assembly is designed to help children realise that we are all attached to each other in school. Our behaviour inevitably influences the happiness or otherwise of those around us.

This means that we have a responsibility to be our best selves at all times for the sake of those around us.

Preparation

This assembly may benefit from a rehearsal.

You will need the following:

- Length of about 15 m (50 ft) of thin nylon fishing line. We recommend 5 kg (12 lb) breaking strain. Buy the cheapest available.
- Face-sized piece of thick paper or card with a picture of a face drawn on it.
- Strong sticky tape – gaffer tape if possible.
- This assembly requires a good deal of co-operation from three other teachers. Ask ones who look cheerful.

Just prior to the assembly:

1 Cut off about 1 m (3 ft) of fishing line. Attach this to the paper with the face painted on it. Use the strong sticky tape.

2 Divide the rest of the line into three equal pieces.

3 Prior to the assembly you and your three assistants need to be attached to each other by the line.

4 Number yourselves 1 to 4 (you are 1). You need to be attached to 2, 2 to 3, and 3 to 4. Tie the line around your waists, and try to make the attachments as invisible as possible.

5 Tie the line attached to the face around your wrist.

The assembly

As the children come in, ask them to sit quietly. Stand facing the school, with the paper face on the floor at your feet.

When everyone is settled, start the assembly as usual, in this way.

Good morning, everyone. I am pleased with the way Class 1 came in. You were very quiet today, well done. Robert, please don't lick Nadia. *[You know, the usual sort of stuff.]*

As you speak, wave your arms around so that the face jumps about. After a few moments the children will begin to call out to you, telling you about the face. Pretend you can't understand what they are trying to tell you.

The children near the front will be able to see the fishing line. They will be calling out to tell you that you have the line attached to your hand.

Eventually show that you realise you have the line attached to you. Laugh and make the face dance about even more. Pretend you cannot see the face. Keep laughing as the paper face leaps about.

Now pretend you suddenly see the face. Hold the paper up and look at the face. Laugh some more and tell the children you are going to make the face dance all around the room.

You now make horrible faces at the paper face. Say it is an ugly face, a stupid face, and so on. Laugh really unkindly.

You can extend this ghastly behaviour to the limit of your imagination. For instance, imagine this face is a picked-on child and be as vile as you can. This is not easy for teachers, but the more realistically nasty you are, the better. The children will be dreadfully shocked by this behaviour.

Now stop. Stand in front of the school, dangling the face by the fishing line.

Then teacher 2 gets up and speaks.

Oh, I think you are being horrible. I am going away from here.

The three teachers attached to you attempt to walk away, but they can't.

Teacher 3 gets up and says they are going to take the face away from you. As they walk towards you, they pull the attached teachers with them. Carefully, making sure the tape stays attached to the face, they try to take the face from you, but of course the face is attached to your wrist.

Teacher 4 stands up and announces they are going off with teacher 2.

You all now pull in different directions, but you cannot escape each other as you are attached to each other by the line. A little bit of mayhem may now ensue as you all attempt to go in different directions.

You could use lots of 'I don't want to be around you', 'My mum says I am not to play with you because you are horrible', 'That face is coming with me.'

Teacher 1 (you): Where do you think you are going? That face is my friend and knows I'm only joking. I'm not really being horrible. *[Bullies frequently claim to be friends of their victims.]*

You will need to make this part as lifelike as possible.

You (suddenly): Stop! We all seem to be stuck to each other. I don't want to be with you but I can't get away.

The other teachers all say similar things.

You now come out of role and turn to the school. The other teachers will probably have to stand near you – they may be able to sit, if they have not got tangled up with each other. Don't cut them loose; that would undermine the point of the assembly. Continue.

Now, this is just a play. This piece of paper is just that, a piece of paper. But if this face was a real person, how do you think they would be feeling right now?

Take answers from the school. Then explain.

This face is like a person in our school. They got stuck to me by accident. They did not choose to be attached to me. That happens in school. We don't choose who is in our class. We don't choose who is in the same clubs or teams as us. We don't choose who is on our bus. We don't always choose who is lining up next to us.

How they behave towards us can make us feel happy or sad. When people are horrible to us, as I was pretending to be towards this face, it can make us feel terrible.

When it happens to us we sometimes ask for help. Have you ever done that?

Sometimes when we ask for help we are told, 'Just stay away from the horrible person. Keep out of their way. Don't play with them.' Has any one ever been told that? *[Take answers.]*

It's not always possible. In school we are all attached to each other.

Just as these teachers were attached to each other, so we are attached to each other. We have to see each other every day, we have to eat together, line up together, sit next to each other, play games together. We really can't keep very far away from each other.

What can we do about this?

If running away is not an option, we have to stay together and try to sort out our problems. As well as comforting the bullied, we also have to learn to talk to bullies.

Winston Churchill, a famous prime minister of the United Kingdom, once said: 'Jaw jaw is better than war war.' That means talking is better than fighting.

So let's take our disputes to circle time or to the school council, or discuss them together. However we do it, we must do it in the right way. We must:

O treat others as we would like to be treated

O forgive each other

- learn to share
- be kind and helpful
- be honest with ourselves about our part in problems
- listen to each other
- do our best to be our best selves.

We must remember we are all in this school together. We can't just run away.

Prayer

Dear Lord, help us to love one another as you love us. Help us to remember that we all need to be treated with kindness. You told us to treat other people as we would like to be treated. So let us treat others kindly. Help us also to remember that we must never give back unkindness if others are unkind to us.

Two thoughts for the day

Don't let other people's bad behaviour make you behave badly.

Jaw jaw is better than war war.

I'm a celebrity – leave me on the window ledge

Theme

This assembly encourages children to think about the current cult of celebrity. An interest in the lives of celebrities can command too much of our attention, wasting time and energy. The problem is, as Van Morrison said about something else, it is ever present everywhere.

Preparation

You will need these:

- ❂ old Barbie doll
- ❂ if possible, a Ken
- ❂ a few copies of magazines that specialise in the lives of celebrities
- ❂ a few photographs of some real modern heroes: Barak Obama, Sir Ranulph Fiennes, Bear Grylls, Bruce Parry, Dame Kelly Holmes, Jamie Oliver, Ray Mears, Sir Chris Hoy, Christine Ohuruogu, Rebecca Adlington.

Photographs of all these people are available free on Google Images, and you can get information about them from Wikipedia. If you have any ex-pupils whom you consider heroic, get some pictures of them – especially old school photographs where they looked just like any other school girl or boy.

The assembly

Leave the doll(s) at the side of the hall, close to hand but out of sight.

Good morning, everybody. I have some great news! I have brought along to school a real celebrity. This celebrity is really famous. Thousands of people have seen her; indeed, she is looked at by hundreds of people every day.

Would you like to meet a real celebrity? You would? Well, it's nearly time.

Who can think of some celebrities? Let's have some names. *[You may find some of the younger children will be at a loss here. The older children will have no trouble naming countless celebrities. You will probably have no clue about who these people are.]*

As each name is mentioned, ask how many people have heard of the person and then ask why they are famous. Ask a nearby member of staff to write down the name of each and why they are famous.

Well, we know a good few celebrities, don't we? I have brought along a magazine or two that tell me all about celebrities. Listen to some of this.

Now read out some of the more pointless stories. Don't read out names; just read what is said about the people mentioned – for example, this one is seen in a horrible skirt, that one has a new girlfriend, this one has put on weight, that one has a new hairdo – the usual pointless trivia. If you know nothing about such magazines, a quick trip to the supermarket or corner shop will soon enlighten you.

Well, that was interesting, wasn't it? How do you know they are celebrities? What is the definition of celebrity?

Take several suggestions: lots of people have heard of them, they are seen all over the place, they are famous, they are fashionable, they are on television, they are in magazines, and so on.

Now it's time to meet today's celebrity. Here she is. Ta Da! My old Barbie.

She is a celebrity. She fits the bill. Lots of people have seen her. She has been sitting on my windowsill for years and everyone who passed by my house saw her. That must be lots of people every day. She is fashionable, she loves clothes, millions of people have heard of Barbie, she is on television and in adverts, she is in lots of magazines, and she is all over the world.

This doll is a celebrity! But what has she ever done? *[Pause for suggestions.]*

Nothing.

She has never done anything at all. She has never been kind, she has never helped anyone, she has never given up something she wanted for the sake of someone else, she has never worked hard for something important, she has never shown bravery, she has never shown great talent in creation. Nothing.

But everyone knows Barbie.

Do you think this doll is admirable? Do you think she has done anything we should be impressed by?

No, neither do I.

So whom should we be impressed with? People who are famous for nothing, like Barbie? People who are famous because they are rich, or are married to someone rich? People who are famous because they are thin or pretty or just like being photographed? Or should we make more effort and choose our celebrities a bit more carefully?

Some celebrities are good and are worthy of that title

Get your pictures out.

These are some of the people I think are celebrities.

It's OK for these people to be in magazines because they have done a lot of good things.

As you get each one out, say something about why they are justifiably celebrated.

Barak Obama, Sir Ranulph Fiennes, Bear Grylls, Bruce Parry, Dame Kelly Holmes, Jamie Oliver, Ray Mears, Sir Chris Hoy, Christine Ohuruogu, Rebecca Adlington. *[Plus any others you have chosen.]*

So, I am afraid, Barbie, you must go back on the ledge. You are not my heroine.

We can't stop silly magazines being printed or sold. But we can stop buying them, and we can stop being impressed with them.

We can choose whom we admire. Let's make celebrities out of people who deserve to be celebrated.

This week we are going to turn one of the noticeboards into a true celebrity magazine. I want everyone to bring in pictures of people who have done something really wonderful, something that was difficult, something that helped others or something that made the world a better place.

You don't have to be rich, thin, beautiful or on television to be someone we should celebrate. But you do have to do your best with whatever talents and skills you may have and you do have to work really hard.

Any one of us can do that. We can all be celebrities. We can all lead lives that are worth celebrating.

Prayer

Help me, Lord, to be someone who makes a difference to the people around me. Show me how best I can use the talents and skills you have given me. Please help me to be a good and useful person. Lord, please help me to lead a life that is worth celebrating.

Thought for the day

Enjoy celebrity for a useful life well lived – and know that you are worth it.

I'm in with the in-crowd

Theme

This assembly arose when there was a great deal of trouble with girls who all wanted to be in with the 'cool' girls and boys who were being hideously exclusive with the football at lunchtime. These in-crowd children were also busy labelling others as 'sad kids' or 'geeky kids', and so on. This assembly helped them to see that they all had a good deal more in common with each other than they previously realised.

Preparation

You will need:

- ✪ 10 hula hoops
- ✪ 10 paper labels (make them A4 size and laminate them if possible) – they should read: Dance Divas, Simpsons' Squad, MSN Magicians, Team Spirits, Top Linguists, Computer Wizards, Swimming Stars, Swift Skaters, Music Maniacs, Good God Gang

Fix the labels to the hoops with sticky tape.

The assembly

Lay the labelled hula hoops out all over the floor at the front of the hall in which you are doing the assembly. Space them out as much as you can.

When the children come in, ask one whole year group to stand up at the front. We suggest year 5 or 6. If yours is a small school, you may like to include two year groups. You want to aim for about forty children standing at the front.

Good morning, children. This morning I have decided to divide you all up into groups. I thought it would make it easier if I could label you all according to which group you are in.

OK, everyone who likes dancing stand in or by this hoop.

Now anyone who likes *The Simpsons* stand in this hoop. Do we have anyone who likes dancing and *The Simpsons*? Yes. Well, we had better put the hoops slightly over each other so you can stand in both *[as in a Venn diagram]*.

Now let's have anyone who likes using MSN in this hoop. Is there anyone who likes MSN and *The Simpsons* and dancing? Oh dear, this is getting confusing.

Now let's have anyone who is a team spirit – that is anyone who likes football, netball, hockey, basketball or any other team game. You go to your hoop. Oh dear, lots of you also like MSN – oh, and *The Simpsons* too? Oh dear, you are getting in a muddle.

You can try getting them to put different feet in different circles, you can suggest they move from one circle to the next, or get them to try hanging on to others in other circles. It has got to be completely chaotic.

Now let's have the super-linguists in this hoop – that is anyone who speaks a different language at home from what they speak at school.

Is there anyone who speaks more than one language who also belongs in some of these other circles? Oh dear, lots. Gosh, this is getting even worse.

Now let's have the computer experts in this hoop. Do lots of you also belong in other hoops as well?

Do the same for swimmers and skaters. More and more children should be trying to be in lots of circles.

Let's have the music fans here. Oh gosh, that seems to be just about all of you.

There is increasing chaos and confusion. Children by now should be all over the place.

Now let's have any of you who go to church, mosque, synagogue, temple or any other place of worship in this hoop here.

Oh, but all of you also belong in all of these other circles.

Act this up. Look harassed.

Stop! This isn't working! All sit down on the floor wherever you are.

Address them and the whole school.

I thought I could get all of you children neatly divided up.

I thought I could label you all tidily into one group or another. But it doesn't work, does it? I have discovered that you can't label children. You are all too complex for that. You can't be fitted into one group or another.

You all have a great deal more in common with each other than I realised – and maybe more than you realised.

You see, we are connected to each other. We all belong together. There are no exclusive groups in this school – just lots of children enjoying the opportunity to do the things they enjoy together.

Prayer

Dear God, you made us all to be each other's brothers and sisters. Help us to see the things we have in common with each other and not to think we are part of any exclusive group.

Thought for the day

There are no exclusive cliques, gangs or in-crowds here. We all belong to one fabulous group – our school.

I'm part of the team

Theme

Many children want to demonstrate their different allegiances to their teams, hobbies, favourite bands and TV programmes. But let us never forget we belong to a great team called 'Our School'.

Preparation

This assembly is shameless. It is a great big piece of populist self-publicity – but why not? You are a great school.

Planning this assembly may be very easy or very difficult, depending upon your staff, friends, family and size. You need to dress yourself from head to foot in different branded and logo-covered kit and clothing – such as a Chelsea football shirt or a T-shirt with the logo of a really popular band on it, a recent film spin-off baseball cap, branded trainers, Dr Who socks – everything you can lay your hands on.

If you can't find any of the above to fit you – even after consulting with your staff and top year – you could try to find pens, pencils, pencil cases, rucksacks, baseball caps, scarves or water bottles with affiliations to various sports, sporting teams, bands, films and TV programmes – perhaps an Angelina Ballerina umbrella, a Charlie and Lola lunch box, and so on. They must be popular or current or you are going to be lonely on that stage.

Cover yourself with assorted allegiances. If you can, wear a school sweatshirt underneath the football shirt or T-shirt.

You also need a boy and a girl dressed in perfect school uniform. You could have a girl and a boy dressed in perfect school PE kit too, if you have such a thing.

The assembly

After the school has assembled, you should enter, looking utterly ludicrous in all of the assorted gear. With luck, the children will laugh their Simpsons socks off.

The perfectly dressed children need to be sitting in the front row. Do not draw attention to them yet.

Good morning! Do you like my outfit? No?

Who likes some of it?
Who supports my hat? *[Get that child up to the front or on to the stage.]*
Who supports my shirt? *[Get those children up.]*
Who likes the film on my pencil case? *[And so on.]*

Do this until you have a good gang of children up on the stage. If you want, you can tell them they can wear your scarf on stage or hold the pencil case – you might be glad to be relieved of all this while you carry on with the assembly.

Now you need to interview the children who are at the front. Ask them why they like a certain team or sport, what it is they like about this TV programme or that band. Ask the school in general if anyone has other types of kit or film or TV branded clothing or whatever.

Don't denigrate any of these things, whatever you may feel about them. You are just about to give a big plug to the whole idea of using clothing to demonstrate allegiance.

Now thank the children, relieve them of all the assorted gear, and put it down near you.

Well, sometimes we like to tell other people about the things, teams and films, books and TV programmes that we like through wearing things with their name on. Lots of us like many different things.

Today I want to say to all of you that there is something that we can all be really proud of. There is something we can go out in the street wearing that announces that we are special.

That is our school uniform.

Get the tidily uniformed children up at the front or on the stage.

When we wear this we say 'This is my team!' We show everyone we meet that we are part of this great team that is our school.

When we wear this kit at matches at home or away we say 'I am proud to be part of my school team!'

We belong to a great team: Team *[name your school]*.

So, just as we are proud of our Chelsea or Man U shirt or Harry Potter pencil case, we can be proud of our school stuff.

Who can tell me a reason to be proud of our school?

Call out to the front or stage any child with their hand up. Quickly interview them.

Why are you proud of this school? What is the best part of going to this school? What would you miss if you had to leave this school?

When you have done that, get them to sit down near the front.

As we are a special school, filled with special children and special teachers, let us wear our uniform with pride. Let's not forget bits of it and let's keep it clean and neat.

Let's remember we are a great team. We are part of Team *[name your school]*.

Now take off your football shirt or whatever and reveal the school sweatshirt. Encourage applause.

Prayer

Dear Lord, we are proud of our school. Help us to behave well so that our school can be proud of us. And, Lord, we want you to be proud of us. Help us to behave as you would like us to behave. Let us bring honour to your team and your name.

Thought for the day

We may support great teams and great bands. But let us never forget we belong to the best team – it's called Our School.

Just my cup of tea

Theme

Schools, like nations, have to try both to encourage healthy team spirit and to celebrate differences. Sometimes we forget that we can be a good team, yet still allow individuality to flourish. It is of egotistical or selfish individualism that we must be wary.

Preparation

The preparation for this is not arduous, and you may have all the props in the staffroom. You will need the following:

- ✪ Several different types of tea – it may be enough to raid the staffroom cupboard, but you may bring in different teas from home (if you have 'builders' tea' only, you should purchase a couple of packets; you will be able to give them away to grateful staff at the end of the assembly). Apart from Lapsang Souchong, I would use tea bags. If the tea comes from the staffroom, if possible label each packet with the name of its owner to help you identify who likes that tea.
- ✪ As many cups as packets of tea.
- ✪ Table.
- ✪ One or two large Thermos flasks filled with very hot water.
- ✪ Large bowl.
- ✪ Pint of milk.
- ✪ Bowl of sugar.
- ✪ Lemon or bottle of lemon juice (optional).

- ✪ Teaspoon.
- ✪ Jug of cold water.
- ✪ Assistant – use a jolly teacher as a child may spill the tea.
- ✪ Pair of scissors.

The assembly

Before the assembly, make sure you have all the tea packets displayed on the table. Get the cups lined up and be sure the water in the flasks is freshly boiled.

Good morning, everybody. This morning I thought I might make the teachers a nice cup of tea before assembly. I looked in the staffroom cupboard, and look what I found.

[Lift up the packets as you name them.] Redbush tea from South Africa, peppermint tea, blackcurrant, ginseng, Earl Grey, Lapsang Souchong from China, Assam from India, green tea, camomile tea, ginger tea. *[Name the types you have.]*

'Oh, goodness,' I said. 'I can't be bothered with all of that! I just meant who wanted a cup of ordinary tea!' And I left the staffroom thirsty.

But then I got to thinking: perhaps all of these teas are delicious. Maybe if I tasted them I would like them all.

Maybe you would like them all. Shall we see?

May I have an assistant? *[Up comes your jolly teacher.]*

Now you need to make one cup after another. You may have to put a dash of cold water in each cup after the hot water to avoid burning people's mouths.

May we have a volunteer to taste this one? What do you think?

Ask for people to taste all the teas as you make them. Many will hate them – to many people most herb teas taste like pond water – but try to get a fan for each tea. The best way to do that is to use tea that really is from the staffroom and ask the member of staff who owns it to taste it (that is why you have put their name on the box). Be prepared to add milk, sugar or lemon.

After you have had lots of fun with 'Yucks' and 'Yums', stop.

Well, we have found that some people like one and some like another, but no one seems to like all of them.

I know, I will make a cup of tea with all of them in, and then everyone will like that one.

Open several tea bags, pour the contents into the bowl and pour on water from the flask.

OK, we now have a bit of everything in here. That should mean that everyone will like this tea. Oh, I know, some people like lemon *[add lemon].* Some like sugar *[add some sugar]* and some like milk *[put in some milk].*

I've made you a lovely cup of tea.

That should please everyone! Who would like to taste this?

It may be difficult to get volunteers for this. What is worse, you might get the perishing year-4 lad who will undoubtedly know he is supposed to say it is horrible and so will come out and announce 'Yum, it's lovely!' to spoil the whole thing. I would love to say 'There is always one', but in our experience there are always at least six. If you do get a saboteur, then say 'I am glad you like it. Please finish the entire bowlful.' They won't.

Well, that was very interesting.

It seems that there are lots of different types of teas and different people like different ones. It also seems that if I try to make just one variety that will please everybody, I fail.

You know, I think that's like our school. You see, there are lots of different types of people in this school. They are all a bit like these teas.

Look, this one says 'refreshing'. That's like *[name a child].* I have always found they are most refreshing.

This one says 'calming.' Now that is like *[name another child].* If I am stressed I have always found they calm me down.

And this one says 'revitalising.' Now that is like *[name].* They always cheer me up.

Just as we have teas we like best of all, so we often have best friends.

Equally, there are some people we are not so fond of. But that doesn't mean they are horrible people. To someone else they are wonderful. Just like these teas.

We are all different and we all like different things in our friends.

Never say, 'That tea is horrible!' It isn't. To someone else it is delicious.

Never say, 'You are horrible!' They aren't. They are someone else's best friend.

Like the teas, you all have special qualities and some come from far away. But we need the variety you all bring to the school. And, just as trying to mix all the tea together to get one that everyone liked didn't work, trying to make all of you children the same wouldn't work.

You are all different. You are all special. You are all wonderful in your own individual way. That's why in this school we celebrate your differences.

We celebrate your cultural differences. How do we do that? *[Talk about times when you have celebrated Chinese New Year, held special Indian dance days, used steel pans, and so on.]*

We celebrate your religious differences. *[Talk about Diwali, Hanukkah, Easter celebrations, and so on.]*

We celebrate your different talents. *[Talk about sports days, school plays, concerts, art exhibitions and swimming galas.]*

In fact, we make sure that in this school no one is left out. Everyone is celebrated.

Like the teas, everyone is different, but everyone is truly delicious in their own unique way.

Prayer

Dear Lord, you made each of us to be unique. Help us to appreciate the good in others, however different from us they may be.

Thought for the day

In this school no one is left out. Everyone is celebrated. Everyone is different but everyone is truly delicious in their own unique way.

More lessons from fishing

Theme

Even in times of economic uncertainty there are children who cause all kinds of distress and jealousies in school through boasting about their possessions. It is always upsetting to see how many children feel that you need to have 'stuff' in order to enjoy life, and that the more you have, the more successful you will be. If we are to create an inclusive school we must do our best to stamp out divisive materialism. We have to show children that the right attitude can triumph over reliance on possessions.

Preparation

You need:

- ✪ two adults
- ✪ two stools to sit on, but if no stools are available, just stand up – you will not be getting around to doing any actual fishing
- ✪ a mobile phone.

If you can, lay a long piece of blue paper (or fabric) across the front of the stage. It should look like a river.

This is one of those assemblies where you can go right over the top with kit. The idea is that two of you look like real fishing enthusiasts. If you have masses of fishing gear, hats, coats, waders even, get togged up. If you don't, a jacket each will be fine. And if you happen either to have lots of fancy fishing tackle at home or know someone who has some, all to the good. If not, rely on mime skills.

We suggest you write the complicated descriptions of tackle on a sticky label and stick it on the palm of your hand so that you can read it. Alternatively attach it to the rods if you are lucky enough to have some. Don't try to remember what to say. Unless you are a real fishing buff, you will forget. You won't be able to blag it because there are bound to be children in your school who could fish for Britain.

Don't forget: the secret of all good assemblies is never the accoutrements; it is your enthusiasm. That just happens to be the theme of this assembly.

The assembly

You and your fellow angler are standing chatting inaudibly to each other as the children come in. Once they are all assembled, you can begin. You do no fishing.

You: I wonder where Jack is. He said he would be here by now. He can't be held up by having to collect his tackle.

You both laugh – not very kindly.

Mollie: Hardly! He only has an old stick and a bent pin. Not like us. We have got some terrific kit!

You: Oh, the best. Would you like to see my new rod? Look at this. It's carbon fibre, much lighter than the old rod. It's got Superlight SIG guides for maximum tip speed recovery. And resistance-free rings for effortless line glide. It has no flat spots and it's got a magnificent power curve.

Mollie: That's amazing! How much did it cost?

You: It was £280. It's the very best. I always buy the most expensive equipment.

Mollie: Well, that's fantastic! Would you like to see my new reel? It's got the best high-speed gearing, the latest oscillation and drag systems and a one-way floating clutch. It gives perfect line lay and has a long cast spool. And it's got ten stainless-steel bearings!

You: Wow, that's incredible! How much did that set you back?

Mollie: £260. But you have to pay for the best.

You: Oh, I agree. I have spent loads of money on this fishing game.

Mollie: So have I. I think I have spent even more than you have. I get all my tackle from the top suppliers in London.

You: I get all of mine from a really exclusive shop in Scotland.

If you are wearing fancy hats, coats, waders, and so on, you can now start boasting about all that. 'My coat cost £400 but it's got elk-bone buttons and a secret pocket for my solid-silver personalised hip flask' – you know the kind of toe-curling bragging stuff that's appropriate. Lay it on really thick.

Mollie: I wonder where Jack is. You know how keen he is. Always practising his casting with that stick and bent pin of his.

You: He should be here by now. I wish he would hurry up. Oh, wait a minute, my phone is buzzing in my pocket.

Hello? Jack? Oh, hi, where are you? Your car has broken down? You can't get here? Oh dear. But you have walked to the river near you and caught loads of fish. OK. Bye then.

Put the phone back in your pocket.

You: He can't get here.

Mollie: Shame.

You: Thing is, there's not much we can do now.

Mollie: Why not?

You: We forgot the bait and we can't buy any round here. We are going to have to pack this lot up and go home. He's got the worms and the maggots.

You both go off together, muttering.

Mollie: Did you say he had caught loads of fish?

You: Yes, with his old stick and bent pin – and his bait.

Now come back to centre stage as yourself.

Those two were a real pair of idiots, weren't they? They missed the point of fishing. The point of fishing is to catch fish. They had forgotten that it was really important to bring bait. They didn't need fancy rods and reels – they needed bait.

We do this kind of thing sometimes: we forget the real point and get caught up in 'stuff'.

Who really likes running on sports day? *[They will probably nearly all respond.]*

What makes a good runner? *[Take answers throughout.]*

That's right; you need to train and to keep fit. You have to be careful what you eat so you don't get too heavy.

Do you need a good amount of sleep?

Should you eat lots of sweets?

To be a good runner you have to be fit, you have to eat good food, you have to get plenty of sleep and you have to train.

Does having fancy trainers make you a good runner?

No, of course not. What would happen if you remembered the fancy trainers but forgot to train?

Yes. You would be hopeless.

What about drawing? If I give you a box of expensive crayons and expensive paper, will that mean you will be good at art? No.

Who likes drawing and painting? What helps you to be good at art? It takes practice, looking carefully at what you draw and even more practice. Plus a good teacher.

Use as many examples as you can, such as the following.

Fancy maths equipment won't help if you have forgotten to learn your tables.

An expensive stove won't make you a good cook if you have neglected to buy fresh ingredients.

An elaborate keyboard won't make you a good pianist if you have forgotten to do your piano practice.

An amazing fountain pen won't make you into a good writer if you have forgotten to learn your spellings.

So, let us remember that it's what we bring to an activity that helps us to do it well, not buying fancy equipment.

We have to bring our hard work, diligence, enthusiasm and persistence. Those qualities are a lot more useful than any amount of stuff – and they won't cost a penny.

Prayer

Dear Lord, please help us to remember that it is not the things we own or buy that will help us to be the people you made us to be, but our hard work, diligence, enthusiasm and persistence. Please be with us as we work to develop these skills.

Thought for the day

Let us remember this:

> *It's not the kit that makes you fit,*
> *Just owning stuff is not enough,*
> *It's endeavour*
> *That will help to make you clever.*

No, thank you, I can manage

Theme

Sometimes we are too proud to accept help when we need it, and too proud to allow ourselves to be taught.

Preparation

Not much – you will need these:

- ✪ needle and thread
- ✪ button
- ✪ needle threader (there is usually one in a packet of needles)
- ✪ something that you can sew a button on – use any unwanted piece of material (it needs to be large enough to look like a garment) or get a cheap item of clothing from a charity shop (sometimes, if you explain what it is for, they will give you something from the stockroom that is too tatty to sell)
- ✪ four willing volunteers – they can be a mixture of staff and pupils:
  - Volunteer 1 needs to be competent at sewing on a button.
  - Volunteer 2 needs a pair of reading glasses.
  - Volunteer 3 needs the needle threader.
  - Volunteer 4 needs a small pair of scissors – nail scissors would be fine.
- ✪ humility – you are going to look a bit of a clown in this assembly! In fact you need to behave badly.

This is one of those assemblies in which you have to act like one of the worst-behaved children in the school. In this instance you need to be stroppy, ungracious and bad tempered. For some of us perhaps that is not too great a stretch. You can play this for laughs – there is nothing funnier than a teacher behaving like a foot-stamping Violet Elizabeth Bott.

The assembly

The assembly opens with you sitting on a chair with some sewing on your knee.

Good morning, children. As you can see, I have a bit of a problem this morning. I wanted to wear this jacket/cardigan/coat/skirt *[whatever]*, but it's missing a button.

Now, as I have always told you children, it is very important that you look smart at all times. You must not go around in tatty clothes. I had better make sure that I am not wearing something with a button missing.

Oh dear! I am having trouble threading this needle, however.

Try a few times, making sure you are acting in a way that demonstrates that you are getting quite cross because you cannot thread the needle. Eventually Volunteer 1 speaks.

Volunteer 1: Would you like me to help you?

You refuse the help in a bad-tempered and ungracious manner.

No, thank you. I can manage quite well on my own. I am just finding it a bit difficult to see. I left my glasses at home.

Volunteer 2 offers to lend you their reading glasses. Again you refuse the offer of help in a very irritable, not to say rude, manner.

No, thank you. I said I could manage, didn't I?

You carry on trying, getting increasingly bad tempered and making no progress. Eventually Volunteer 3 speaks.

Volunteer 3: I have a needle threader in my bag. I could show you how to use it, if you like.

No, thank you. I said I can manage quite well without any help. I don't need anyone telling me what to do. You can all just leave me alone!

After a couple more minutes of trying, you stand up and speak in a really fed-up, maybe even tearful, tone.

It's no good, I can't do it. I am rubbish at sewing anyway. I don't care. I will just throw the silly old jacket/cardigan/coat/skirt away!

Start to walk away. Then stop and address the children, still acting in a rather emotional way:

That isn't really true, though. I do like wearing that jacket/cardigan/coat/skirt. What I don't like is accepting help or having people show me how to do things. I don't like people thinking they are cleverer than me or trying to boss me about.

The trouble is, the only person who is losing out here is me. I am not going to get to wear my nice clothes. *[You think for a second or two.]*

I think I have been a bit silly. Maybe I will ask those kind people if they will help me after all.

Excuse me *[addressing the volunteers]*, I am sorry I was such a grump. I would like a bit of help after all.

Volunteer 3 (with the needle threader): **Of course, I'd love to help.** *[They come out and instantly thread the needle. When they have finished they speak again.]* **Keep it for next time, I have several.**

You: **Thank you so much. Actually, I am not very good at sewing.**

Volunteer 3: **No problem! First we need to find where the button goes, then we need to snip off the old cotton.** *[Looks up.]* **Does anyone have a small pair of scissors?**

Volunteer 4 cheerfully calls out that they do. They bring them up to the front (carrying them in the best 'how to walk with scissors' fashion).

Volunteer 3 snips off the old cotton and quickly sews the button on, explaining how to do it as they go. When it is done you continue.

Thank you, all of you. You have been so helpful. I really couldn't have managed on my own. I don't know where I would be without help.

All the volunteers go back to their seats. You address the school.

Did I behave very well at first? No? What did I do that was silly? *[Take suggestions.]*

I think you are right. I was a bit silly, wasn't I?

Do any of you ever hate asking for help? *[Look for hands up.]*

Why? *[Again, take suggestions from the school.]*

You are right, sometimes it is difficult to ask for help and sometimes it is difficult to accept help when it is offered. We may think that we look silly if we ask for help, or we may feel that people only want to help us so they can boss us about. Sometimes we don't want to ask for help because we feel that the person we ask will think they are cleverer than us.

Why else don't we like asking for help? *[Take more suggestions from the school.]*

If we never have any help with things we find difficult, what happens? *[Take more suggestions.]*

So, if we have a problem with something, what is the grown-up, sensible thing to do? *[Again get suggestions.]*

I think you are right. We should graciously accept help when we need it.

I think you children are all very clever. I was a bit silly and I nearly had to throw away my favourite jacket/cardigan/coat/skirt.

So from now on let us all remember this. The sensible person asks for help when they need it and accepts help when it's offered.

We can all help each other. Children and teachers can all help each other.

We are a school that knows how to help each other and to work together.

Prayer

Dear God, help us not to be too proud to accept help. Let us be helpful towards others and learn to accept help from others.

Thought for the day

Humility is the lamp that lights the way to learning.

Let's all go nuts together

Theme

The aim of this assembly is to help children understand that we are all different both on the outside and on the inside, but it is what is on the inside that really matters.

Preparation

Before you do anything else, check that you don't have any children in school who are so allergic to nuts that they can't even be in the same room as a nut in its shell. If you do, you can't hold this assembly.

There is nothing too arduous about planning this assembly. You need a large bag of mixed nuts in their shells: hazel nuts, walnuts, Brazil nuts, almonds, and so on. These are available in the winter from most big supermarkets. They must be mixed varieties and they must be in their shells. (A bag of mixed nuts grabbed at the pub the night before just won't work.)

The assembly

A word of warning: any assembly about nuts asks for lots of jokes about nutty children, Mr Jenkins who is a sports nut and Miss Atkins who is nuts about George Clooney, and so on. Whilst tempting, singling people out with witty remarks is not quite in the spirit of the assembly.

I was digging in my garden / window box / the grounds of my large country estate at the weekend when I found a hazel nut. At first I was quite excited. I wiped the mud off the shell and admired its beautiful colour and markings.

Then I noticed that it had a hole in it, and I realised that it had been eaten by a squirrel. It was beautiful but useless.

I dug around a bit more and found another one. This had not been eaten. I took it inside and washed it, then got out my nut crackers and cracked it. Oh, the disappointment! Inside there was nothing but dust. That was why the squirrels had left it: it was useless.

I washed my hands, made a cup of tea and had a good think about nuts in general.

Then I went to the supermarket, bought this bag of nuts *[hold it up]* and brought it into school.

Call up some children and teachers. They need to look very different from each other – for example, a tall year-6 girl, a blond boy, a dark-haired girl, a tiny year 1, a teacher. In all call up about four or five children and adults.

Now you need to ask the school how these people all differ from each other on the outside. They are tall, small, have brown eyes, have fair hair, and so on. (You will have to use tact when someone says of the teacher that they are old, especially if they are about 26.)

Talk about what you know of what goes on inside these people: their likes and dislikes, their skills and talents, their hobbies and enthusiasms. Also talk about their good qualities, their kindness, their ability to be a good friend, their diligence, and so on.

Now you can say to the children that these people are all different on the outside and different on the inside. Explain that this is just like the nuts.

Send the volunteers back to their seats.

Show the school each of the nuts, and ask the children to describe them. Talk about how different they all look. Point out how beautiful they look.

You can then tell them that each of these nuts is also different on the inside, and the most important part of the nut is what is found inside. It is the inside that feeds us and that feeds the seedling if we plant the nut. If the nut is empty inside it is useless, no matter how beautiful it looks outside.

The same goes for people. It is what is on the inside of us that matters most.

We wouldn't be much use to the world if we were like either of the nuts you found in your garden. We wouldn't be any good if we were hollow.

Ask the children to remember that the outside of a person is interesting and may even be very beautiful (just think of George Clooney), but we mustn't get carried away by appearances. Just as it's the inside of a nut that is most important, so it is the inside of a person that really matters.

Prayer

Dear Lord, you know what is on the inside of each of us. You care about what is on the inside of each of us. Please help us to look further than the outside of a person. Help us to get to know each other. It takes time and a great deal of listening to come to know a person really well. Help us to find that time and do that listening.

Thought for the day

Just as it's the inside of a nut that is most important, it is the inside of a person that really matters.

Our school is the pick of the bunch

Theme

This assembly arose after a child racially abused another child. When he was questioned it became apparent that the miscreant had a) no idea what any of the abusive terms he was using meant and b) wasn't even aware that the child he was abusing came from another country. He had simply learned from outside school that you could 'wind up' black, Chinese, Pakistani or Indian children by calling them certain names and shouting 'Go home!' We felt it was an appropriate moment to address the issue.

Preparation

This is what you need:

- ✪ As big a vase of mixed flowers as you can afford – supermarkets are a good source of bouquets, but if you have more to spend you could go to a florist. A selection from the flowers listed below would be suitable (you will not be able to buy all of these at the same time).
- ✪ A couple of pot plants (optional) – African violet, cyclamen, lavender and poinsettia are all suitable.
- ✪ To find out where flowers that are not listed below come from, we recommend: http://www.4to40.com/encyclopedia/default.asp – scroll down to 'Flowers'.
- ✪ Address labels – write the name of each flower and its country of origin on an address label and attach it to the stem of the flower so you will have the information you need during the assembly. Don't trust to memory – it is bound to fail at the crucial moment, unless you are a very young teacher.

Some examples of flowers and their origins.

Alstroemeria – Peru
Anemone – Israel
Carnation – Greece, Near East
Chrysanthemum – China, Japan
Cosmos – Mexico
Daffodil – Spain, Portugal
Dahlia – Mexico, Central and South America
Delphinium – tropical Africa
Dog rose – Siberia, China, Japan
Forget-me-not – New Zealand
Forsythia – east Asia
Freesia – South Africa, Sudan
Gerbera – South Africa
Gladiolus – South Africa
Lily – Japan, China, Balkans
Rhododendron – Nepal
Rose – Middle East (Iran, Iraq, Turkey, etc.)
Sweet pea – Crete, Sicily
Tuberose – East Indies
Tulip – Afghanistan, India, Kazakhstan, Turkey

Pot plants
African violet – Tanzania, Kenya
Cyclamen – Spain, France, Italy, Greece, Iran, Turkey, north-east Africa
Lavender – Mediterranean (France, Spain, Italy), north and east Africa
Poinsettia – Mexico

The assembly

The following script shows you how to present this assembly. Adapt it to make it appropriate to what you are using.

I was in my office yesterday and I realised that I was feeling a bit gloomy. I looked about and thought 'This place is dull. It needs something alive in it. It needs colour and life.' So after school I went to *[name shop / garden centre / plant nursery / supermarket]* and bought these beautiful flowers. While I was there I also bought these lovely pot plants.

I came into school with them this morning, put them in my room, and suddenly everywhere looked much better – really bright, cheerful and lively.

You can find flowers like these in any flower shop or supermarket. But you know what? None of them is native to the United Kingdom. That means that originally they came from another country. Most of them now grow here because people brought the plants or seeds to Britain, sometimes a long time ago.

As you talk about each flower, take it out of the vase and show it to the children, like this.

This one is a rose. Originally roses came from countries such as Iran and Iraq.

And this is a chrysanthemum. Many years ago someone brought a chrysanthemum plant from the Far East – it first grew in China and Japan.

Go through your entire collection, naming the flowers and telling the school where each originally grew. Then do the same with the pot plants, if you have any.

Isn't that amazing? All these beautiful flowers that you can find all over the country, in most supermarkets, originally grew in places that are far away. And now many of them are growing here and looking beautiful wherever they are.

The same applies to these plants. We have them in our gardens and in our homes, and without them we would not have so much colour around.

This has made me think about our school. We have lots of children here. Some of these children or their families originally came from far away, like the flowers.

We have children who came here from Somalia, Pakistan or India, and from China, Japan or the West Indies.

Name the countries that apply to your school. If there is a child from an unusual location, you could draw attention to that (e.g. for an Afghan child, explain that they may have come from the mountains of the Hindu Kush, like the tulip).

Like these flowers, these people now belong here. Like most of the flowers, they now grow here. And, like the flowers, people have brought much beauty. They have wonderful music and art for us to enjoy. They have brought impressive celebrations and religious festivals as well as amazing weddings.

Like these flowers, they make our country brighter, more beautiful and more exciting.

If I took all of the 'foreign' flowers from this vase, this is what I would have left.

Put the flowers to one side.

Nothing. The room would be dull again.

And if we lost all of the people in our school who originally came from far away places, our school would be much duller.

So let's be really pleased we are such a wonderful mixed bunch in this school.

Try to finish with one flower from an unusual location, like this.

You know, I should very much like to know someone whose family, like this rhododendron, originally came from the mountains of Nepal. There is a gold star for the first person who finds the country on a map and shows it to me by the end of the day.

Prayer

Lord God, you are our creator and you love variety. You made many plants and flowers, many colours and all kinds of landscapes and climates. We thank you, too, for the variety in the cultures of this world. We are grateful that we can share in all this richness in our school.

Thought for the day

Let us celebrate the beauty in all the kinds of people and cultures that we have in our school.

> *The world is so full of a number of things,*
> *I am sure we should all be as happy as kings*
> Robert Louis Stevenson (1850–1894)

The one with the helicopter crisps

Theme

This assembly is very simple. Children often get upset when they are told off for what they consider to be minor infractions of the rules. However, endless minor infractions add up to chaos. What is more, there are some children who begin in childhood a lifetime of complaining that they are being picked on because they find it hard to accept criticism for minor, but annoying, misdemeanours.

One of the main reasons for children becoming disaffected is that they don't understand why what they are doing is wrong and start to feel in trouble all of the time. This may lead to the child being labelled 'naughty' and the child responding to this label.

The aim of this assembly is to show that rules are there for a reason. If you get into trouble, it may be that you are doing something acceptable but in the wrong place or at the wrong time, rather than being intrinsically bad. Understanding this frequently stops children from feeling got at by teachers, and helps to prevent disaffection.

Preparation

This is quick and fairly simple. Each of the numbered pieces of text below needs to be displayed on its own sheet of card to make eleven pages.

The assembly

Yesterday as I was walking around school I started to get very confused. Everything seemed to be going on in the wrong place.

I was just going along the corridor after registration when I heard the sound of rushing water coming from the boys' cloakroom. I looked in and saw there was a year-2 boy washing his hands. He had the tap on too fast and he was splashing water all over the floor. I was a bit cross. I said, 'Now look what you have done. You have got water all over the floor when it should be in the sink.'

When it was time for assembly I noticed two year-6 girls sitting in the back row talking to each other when they should have been sitting in silence. I said, 'You two girls are not supposed to be talking now. You know you should be silent. This is the wrong place for a conversation.'

Later, when the bell went for lunch and everyone went outside, I just happened to look into a classroom and I saw a girl eating a banana. I told her, 'You shouldn't be doing that here. You should wait until it's your turn for lunch and eat it in the dining hall. You are eating it in the wrong place.'

Then a most surprising thing happened. I found a teacher walking down the corridor with a cup of coffee. 'Oh dear,' I said, 'That is not safe! Suppose a child bumped into you. They would get covered in hot coffee. That should really be drunk in the staff room. You are drinking it in the wrong place.'

In the afternoon I looked out of the window and saw a man delivering new school books. I was very pleased to see him as we have been waiting for them for ages. But then I saw he was parking his van in the minibus parking spot. I rushed outside and said, 'You can't park there! There will be nowhere for the minibus to go when it gets back. You are parking it in the wrong place!'

Now, these people were not doing bad things. The little boy was washing his hands, the girls were talking, the girl by herself was eating a banana, the teacher was drinking coffee and the driver was parking his van. They were the right things, but they were doing them in the wrong place.

Now, I am going to ask eleven children to come out here and stand in a line. I am going to give each of you a card with words on. You are going to read them out.

Ask eleven children to come out to the front. Make sure they are good readers. Stand the children in a line and ask them to read out the words on their cards.

It is vital to ensure the children read the cards out in the order given below (or something similar) and not in the numbered order.

1 A boy walked into a

5 helicopter

8 'We don't

10 crisps. We

7 'Sorry,' said the shopkeeper,

9 have any helicopter

3 asked for some strawberry laces

11 only have plane!'

2 sweet shop and

4 and a packet of

6 crisps.

This joke isn't behaving itself. There is nothing wrong with the words, but they are not where they should be.

Just like the children and the teacher and the van driver, they are doing the right thing in the wrong place.

Every bit of the joke is important, but it needs to be more orderly.

Let's see if we can put it all into the right place.

Reorder the words according to the numbers on the cards. Now read them out.

A boy walked into a sweet shop and asked for some strawberry laces and a packet of helicopter crisps. 'Sorry,' said the shopkeeper, 'We don't have any helicopter crisps. We only have plane!'

OK, it's a bit of a groan joke, but it works a great deal better when the words are in the right place. When it is more orderly, it works better.

We sometimes complain when we are told off, and say we are not doing anything wrong. We say something like 'I'm just talking to my friend', 'I'm just eating a banana', 'I'm just parking my van.'

And we are right. They are not wrong things to do. We are just doing them in the wrong place.

So let us remember that, like the joke, we work better when we are more orderly.

Prayer

Dear Lord, you have provided us with many enjoyable things to do. Eating and drinking and laughing and joking are some of them. Help us to know the right times and places to do them. We want to be a blessing, not a blight, to our school.

Thought for the day

Let's remember that doing the right thing, at the right time, in the right place, may help the world turn a little more easily, and help us to be a blessing, not a blight, to our school.

Traveller or tourist?

This is a leavers' assembly.

Theme

Primary years are principally a time of preparation. A school's job is to prepare children for their journey through their school life and for the adults they will become. In school we may forget some of the very important things children will need. At the same time, we need to help the children to pack light or the journey will be too arduous. School needs to prepare each of the children for their own particular journey.

Preparation

You will need a rucksack (or similar bag) big enough to contain:

- ✪ compass
- ✪ map
- ✪ tube of glue
- ✪ something related to a skill or talent you may have – such as violin bow, dancing shoe, paint brush, football boot, sheet of music
- ✪ kitchen timer
- ✪ charity collection envelope or box
- ✪ large leaf (or a small piece of an evergreen shoot, if it is winter)
- ✪ a few really large stones or big flints (these do not go into the rucksack)
- ✪ string of bunting or blown-up balloon
- ✪ long list, folded up (to make this, cut a piece of A4 into three lengthwise and stick the pieces together to make a strip – the longer you make this, the better; you may either write a real list on the paper or you can just write wriggly lines – that depends how near you are going to be to the children

✪ short list, about eight lines long.

Put all of these items into a box, along with the rucksack.

The assembly

Good morning, children.

I am going on a holiday this summer and I have been thinking about what to pack. I made a list. *[Produce the long list. Wait for the laugh – the longer the list, the longer the laugh.]*

I think I have thought of rather too much, don't you? If I take all of this, I am going to get very tired carrying it around in my rucksack. *[Produce rucksack.]*

After I wrote this list I remembered my friend who always says you should travel light because then you can go further.

So I sat down and made a new list. *[Produce short list.]*

I think this will be better. I will be able to travel further if I follow this list.

You see, I want to be a traveller, not a tourist.

A tourist goes to a place, looks around and then comes home.

A traveller goes to a place and joins in with the life of that place. They go to all sorts of out-of-the-way places and get to know the locals. When they leave that place people miss them.

Planning for my holiday made me think about your lives when you leave this school.

You see, we want to prepare you for the journey of your life. You might think that school is just about lessons, but the lessons are really quite a small part of everything you learn in school.

You have to get ready to be a traveller throughout your life, not just a tourist. You should travel far and make a difference so that when you leave people miss you.

So here is my list for your life's journey. These are some of the things I think you need to put into your rucksack as you travel on.

First you will need a compass. *[Get out the compass and hold it up.]*

We have tried to give you a compass inside you so when you meet difficult situations you will know what to do.

In this school we have taught you to:

treat other people as you would like to be treated
forgive
be kind and helpful
be honest
share
listen
always do your best to be your best self.

That is the compass in your heart.

We shall put this compass in the rucksack. When you come to difficult times or choices in your life, you can get out the compass in your heart and make sure you are going in the right direction. If you follow our school way you will not go far wrong.

Now, the next thing is a map. *[Get out the map.]* That is so you can remember always to have a good look around and not miss anything nearby – like opportunities. Some people never miss an opportunity to miss an opportunity – don't be like those. Always have a good look round and see what you can do to make a difference.

Next out is the glue. This is to help you be sure to stick at things in life.

Now in my rucksack I have put *[get out the object related to the skill or talent you have]* because I like . . . Each of you has skills and talents of your own. At this school we have given you time to develop those. Never forget the things you are good at and be sure to enjoy doing them all of your life.

Ah, now we have this. *[Pull out the kitchen timer.]* It is a kitchen timer. Sometimes we have to learn something called 'delayed gratification'. That's a long way of saying that we have to learn to wait for things sometimes. Delayed gratification involves learning to save up our pocket money for things we want to buy, instead of borrowing from our parents, and it's why we don't spoil surprises for ourselves or other people. It's why we work for exams that we will need to pass to help us in the future. It's important to learn to work and wait for the reward.

Next we have this Christian Aid envelope *[or whatever – hold it up].* We should remember to give away some of our money. There are many people who need it more than we do. It's also why we buy Fairtrade foods, like chocolate. *[Put it in the rucksack.]*

Oh, and here we have a leaf. *[Hold it up.]* It's very important to take time to look at the world around us. There is much to amaze us. We should thank God every day for giving us such a wonderful world. If ever we feel fed up, we can try going for a walk in a garden or a park or the countryside. That will help to cheer us up. *[Put this in the rucksack.]*

Now we come to these rocks. *[Show them to the children.]* There are some things we don't want to carry with us – things like remembering when someone was horrid to us, or when we felt silly because we got something wrong in class, or times when we felt left out. We won't take those things with us because they will just weigh us down. We'll dump them now. *[Put them in the waste bin.]*

That just leaves this. *[Pull out the bunting or balloon.]* This will remind us that it is also very important to have a good time – to have parties and to celebrate things. We mustn't forget to enjoy ourselves. *[Put it in the rucksack.]*

Now that is not too much stuff in the rucksack. I think it will do for the journey. These are some of the things this school has given you for your journey.

We can't all be clever, we can't all be beautiful, and we can't all be good at games, but we can all be travellers through our life, not just tourists. Don't forget to take your rucksack in your heart when you leave us and don't forget that you can make a difference to the world.

Prayer

Dear Lord, life is a long and winding road. Help us to enjoy our journey along it. Help us to appreciate all the beauty and all the friendship we encounter, and help us to forgive those who upset us. Let us celebrate and thank those who care for us, and for others, as we travel along the way.

Thought for the day

Let us prepare for the journey ahead. Let us get ready to be travellers through life and not tourists. Help us to remember to try to make a positive difference everywhere we go, so that when we leave people will miss our contribution. Let us travel light through life, but let us travel with enthusiasm.

But it's only a rabbit!

Theme

This is an assembly about meat. This is a difficult theme. Children need to think about what they eat and consider the ethics of food. You may have vegetarian children in your school; some perhaps have made a decision about that for themselves and some may come from vegetarian families and therefore not have thought about it for themselves. There is no conclusion to this assembly; it is designed to promote thought.

Subsequent discussions on the subject may be held in school. For example, in RE the children could find out which faiths forbid the eating of meat (e.g. Hinduism and Jainism) and why. In PSHE they could investigate the wider concept of animal welfare. There is a good deal of material on the Internet – some of it put there by celebrity chefs with a conscience – that may be useful.

If you are a vegetarian, you will have to adjust this assembly.

Preparation

You need some rabbit meat. This is not difficult to get. You also need a free-range chicken and a battery chicken, ready for cooking. Try to make sure the two chickens look much the same as each other.

The assembly

Good morning, children. How was your weekend? *[Take answers.]* Mine was a little upsetting. You see, on Saturday afternoon I was with a friend who was driving us out into the countryside for an outing. Suddenly a rabbit ran out in front of the car, and she hit it. I was really upset.

She stopped the car and we dashed over to the rabbit. But it was too late. It was dead. We carefully picked it up and laid it down on the bank at the side of the road.

Just then a man cycled past us. And do you know what happened? He stopped and said, 'That's a waste of a good rabbit.'

We replied that we knew that and we were very sorry, but it was an accident.

He said that was not what he meant. He told us he was just off with his ferret to catch a rabbit. If we hadn't knocked that rabbit over, he would perhaps have caught it and taken it home to put in a pie.

I was shocked. 'Oh,' I said, 'how could you do such a thing? How could you kill a poor little bunny rabbit and put it in a pie?'

'Do you eat meat?' he asked.

'Well, yes, I do,' I said. 'But that's different. I buy it in a supermarket.'

'Someone has to kill it for you. And, what's more, I bet the animals it comes from didn't have such a good life as that rabbit did. The rabbits I catch have run about the fields and had a really happy life. Do you know what sort of life the animals you eat have had?'

That set me thinking. I eat meat most days. My favourite is chicken. I suppose I haven't thought much about what chickens do when they are alive.

Because of this conversation, my friend and I changed our plans. We set off to the supermarket. This is what we bought.

This is rabbit. [Show them the rabbit meat.] I have a good recipe for rabbit stew and I am going to make it this evening.

Is that bad?

Encourage some discussion about this. Many children, especially urban children, are out of touch with the reality of eating meat. They do not associate it with an animal. Many children rarely see a cow close to. They may not even link beef with a cow. Even more of them are likely to fail to connect leather shoes, belts, bags, and so on with animal skins. Rabbits, of course, are different; they are pets and are more familiar to them.

Tomorrow I am going to have chicken. I have two here. They look the same, don't they? They are not the same, though. This one is a free-range chicken and this is a battery chicken. This one cost … *[say what you spent]* and this one …. That's a big difference, isn't it? Do you think they taste different? *[Take answers.]*

Well, the answer is that if you put them in a stew they probably taste the same. The difference is that one has had a good life and one has had a terrible life. I've been doing some research. *[Tell them a little about the life of a battery chicken. Don't give lots of gruesome facts, just enough to make them realise it's not pleasant.]*

I have decided that I will never have another chicken again unless it is a free-range one. It will cost more but I will eat less meat if necessary so I can afford it. That's not too difficult; lots of people never eat any meat at all.

Who here does not eat any meat? *[Briefly interview some vegetarians. Ask them for their reasons: own choice, religion, culture, family, health, and so on.]*

Lots of people think eating meat is fine. Others eat it only if the animal it comes from has had a good life. But as we see, some/many children in this school do not eat meat and that is fine too.

What is not fine is giving the matter no thought. So this week/term/year we are going to be thinking about what we eat.

We'll ask just what roast beef is. We'll think about why we don't eat horse but we do eat lamb. We are going to look into animal welfare, too. And we'll try to find out more about why some children don't eat meat at all.

Saturday was a sad day for that rabbit, but not if it leads us to think seriously and sensibly about the food we eat.

Prayer

Lord, you love and value all animals, which are part of your creation. If we choose to eat meat, help us to think about the life the animal had before it died.

Thought for the day

All animals share our lives on earth, but not all share our freedoms. Let us use our freedom to choose the best lives possible for animals.

Graceland

Theme

This is one of our favourite assemblies. It helps the children and, maybe even more, the adults think about what we really value in school. The difficulty is this: we say there are things we value more than academic ability, but do we really do that? This assembly aims to explore our hidden prejudices and what happens when they are challenged. We have always found it a rather chastening assembly.

Preparation

You will need:

- ✪ packet of sticky gold stars, a couple of sheets of Well Done! stickers, or something of that sort
- ✪ two fake letters in sealed envelopes – they must look official and as if they have arrived in the post.

Ask the school secretary to run in with the second letter when you say the words 'I think we need to reorganise the whole school.'

The assembly

Good morning, children. I have got some congratulations to hand out here. Look, lots of stickers/stars to give out.

I will need the teachers' help here. Who has done a good piece of maths work this week? *[Hand out a few rewards in response to names that are put forward.]*

Who has done a good piece of written work? *[Hand out a few more rewards.]*

Who is good at reading? *[Hand out yet more rewards.]*

Well, that's splendid. Lots of good reading, writing and arithmetic. Just what's wanted in school.

Oh, I have an important letter here. I think I had better open it and read it.

As you read the letter through, look more and more alarmed.

Oh dear. Well, this is very serious. Very serious indeed. Hmmm.

I think I had better explain what has happened.

This is a very important letter from the government. It's from the department of education. It says there is to be a big change in our school.

We are no longer going to focus on maths and English because we have been redesignated as a school for dancing, art and sport. They are particularly looking for gracefulness.

This letter says that instead of the SATs we are used to doing, we are going to have tests in dancing, art and sport.

We have to put you into sets according to how good you are at these subjects and according to how graceful you are.

It also says that teachers who are not graceful and are useless at sport, dance and art may get the sack. Heavens, this is very serious.

I am not sure how well I am going to do. *[Describe yourself.]*

Well, for a start, I had better give out some different stars/stickers.

OK. To whom shall we give the rewards now?

Let's find out who is going to do really well in this new-look school.

We shall start with dancing.

Let's have some names from the teachers. Whom do the staff think deserve stars for this?

Encourage names, boys and girls, of those who are good at dancing, then ask those children out and get everyone to give them a clap. Hand out stars/stickers. Point out that the children are not only good at dancing but are also graceful.

Do the same with sport and art. It is important that you do this seriously. Sport, art and dance are important subjects.

'Gracefulness' is meant to be rather vague. It can be applied to the quiet child who is gentle and has beautiful manners and the child who is deft.

Now turn to the teachers.

To which teachers shall we give some claps? Which of our teachers are good at sport, dance and art? Who are the most graceful?

Nominate some teachers and bring them out for praise.

Only say the following if it is blindingly obvious that it applies to you.

I am a little worried. You see, maybe I am not the best person to be the headteacher any more. Perhaps someone who is more graceful than I am should be the head?

Now let's think about the timetable. How much time do we spend on numeracy and literacy? *[The staff should give the exact amounts of time.]*

How much time do we spend on art and dance and sport? *[Again take answers from staff – and pupils, if appropriate.]*

Perhaps we should do two hours of dance and art every day and just do maths and English for half an hour each on Friday afternoons.

Well, this is most interesting. I think we need to reorganise the whole school.

At this signal the secretary comes in with the second letter. You take it, open it and say the following.

Oh dear! That first letter was a mistake. We are not changing. The tests are still going to be for literacy and maths.

During the next part of the assembly get the children to think carefully about what difference it would have made to their lives if the letter had been correct, and respond to the questions below. Ask someone to write down the answers they make.

Who is disappointed?

Who thought they would have enjoyed school more if our school celebrated gracefulness, dance, art and sport? Why?

Who would have been the new school heroes?

Who would have suddenly found school less enjoyable? Why?

Would this new system have been fair?

Is our usual system any fairer?

Should our school appreciate and include all children?

What can we do to make that happen?

Over the coming week try to find ways to put these suggestions into action. Possible ways to do this are art noticeboards; 'colours' for posture, dance and art; sport and/or dance displays; claps in class and assembly for good art work; art and dance homework each week; art and dance discussion at parents' evenings; discussions about table manners and good manners in general; discussions about what gracefulness is; and so on.

Remember, we are all in school for a great many years and we have all been given different talents and abilities. No one talent or ability is any better than another. We want everyone in this school to be a star, so we need to be sure we give equal weight to all talents, abilities and skills.

Prayer

Dear God, all of our lives are lived out in your sight. Let us live gracious lives, valuing in each other the gifts that you have given us, gifts that make us the people you have created us to be. We have our gifts and talents by your grace – your gift to us that we have not earned. Bless us and keep us, make your face shine upon us and be gracious unto us.

Thought for the day

Let us open our eyes to be aware of the beauty of the lives of others.

Not exactly what it says on the tin

Theme

If there has been any kind of teasing of children because of their physical appearance – of those with eczema, psoriasis, thick glasses, Down syndrome, or cerebral palsy, for instance – or children calling each other unacceptable names such as flid, spacky, nigger or paki, now is the time for this assembly.

It is also time to use it if children have been teasing others because they wear different clothes for religious reasons, such as the Muslim headscarf for girls or the Sikh patka for boys.

Preparation

A little preparation is needed here, but nothing too arduous.

You will need:

- ✪ tin opener
- ✪ tin of dog food – what it is must be obvious (e.g. with a picture of a dog on the front) and it must have a ring-pull lid
- ✪ tin of something that looks like dog food but is human food – a tin of cooked steak or mince would be ideal; get a good brand as someone is going to have to eat it
- ✪ plastic can lid designed to fit on the top of an opened tin to keep the contents fresh (you will be fitting it on the bottom of a tin, to keep the steak in) – available in hardware shops or pound shops
- ✪ bowl, plate and fork
- ✪ table to eat at.

You will also need a pre-briefed teacher or pupil. We are always reluctant to use a pupil in case they grin or giggle and give the game away. One suggestion is that you ask your hungriest child; they will be too busy wolfing down the steak/mince to wreck the assembly – boys are always hungry. If no one suitable will take on this role (cold cooked meat may not appeal to anyone and you can't ask many people as that will ruin the surprise), you could use a chocolate Angel Delight with pieces of Mars Bar mixed into it.

This is the complicated bit. You need to open the tin of dog food at the bottom, being careful not to damage the label. Empty the dog food into a bowl and hide it (or give it to a dog). Wash out the dog food tin very carefully, making sure you do not damage the label. Then open the tin of steak in the usual way.

Refill the clean, empty dog food can with the contents of the tin of steak/mince. Put the plastic can lid on the bottom of the dog food can so the contents do not fall out.

Keep the steak tin, but make sure it is out of sight during the assembly.

You now have what looks for all the world like an unopened tin of dog food, but it is in fact a tin of cooked steak/mince.

The assembly

The first part of today's assembly is a bit sad. There have been some unpleasant incidents of name calling in school recently. We don't tolerate that – ever. This is a school for everyone. Anyone who teases someone else because they look different is going to have to come and have a very serious talk with me.

Now for the second part of this assembly.

Turn to Charlie (as we shall call the pre-briefed pupil or teacher, who can be male or female although male is more likely). You need to dispatch them on a mission such as collecting a pencil from the office – anything that gives them a reason to leave the hall. They wait (with a teacher if they are a pupil), just out of sight, until you go to the door and call them. Make sure they come in with whatever you sent them to get.

Oh dear, I seem to have forgotten my pencil. I will need it for this assembly. Charlie, would you go to the office and get a pencil from the secretary? Thank you so much.

Now you speak to the school.

While we are waiting for Charlie to come back, I am going to let you in on a little game I'm going to play. Can you see this tin? What is it?

Hold it up. Let them see that it is a tin of dog food, but don't let them get too close or some eagle eye might spot the lid on the bottom of the tin. Don't say it is dog food – they will make the assumption.

Do you think Charlie would like to eat this? You know s/he is always hungry. What do you think?

Encourage them to call out 'No!' A bit of whipping up of the audience is called for here.

I think s/he will love it! In fact when s/he comes in I am going to give her/him a whole plate of it to eat.

Lay the table. Then, very carefully, in full view of the children, pull back the ring pull and open the can. Very theatrically, empty the tin on to the plate.

Oh, s/he is going to love this! Oh yes, I can't wait for her/him to eat this!

Scrape out the tin carefully. There should be lots of 'Yucks' and vomit noises by now. Don't stop them.

There, a nice plateful for Charlie to eat. He, he!

Go to the door and call.

Charlie, where are you?

Oh, good, here you are. Come back into the hall. I have a special treat for you. As you were so good and went off and collected that pencil, I am going to give you something scrummy to eat.

Sit down here. Here is the fork.

If you are lucky, at this point there will be lots of children calling out 'Don't eat it, Charlie, it's dog food!', and so on. During the briefing you have told Charlie to look at the food and get to work immediately.

Come on, Charlie, ignore them. Is it good? You see, s/he likes it!

All the while s/he is eating, you encourage her/him. Say things like 'Don't listen to them!' You can get the staff to liven the school up if they are too well behaved.

Ideally you will have children nearly fainting with disgust.

When the plate is empty, turn to Charlie.

Well, Charlie, was that tasty?

As it will have been, Charlie will nod enthusiastically.

Any chance of a morsel?

Charlie, the school seem a bit upset about you eating that meat. Ask them why.

S/he does. There will be more calling out, with comments such as 'You have just eaten dog food', 'Charlie, you're going to be sick!', and so on.

Send Charlie to sit down.

Dog food! You all think I have given Charlie dog food to eat? Do you think I would have given her/him dog food? Is that likely? Am I like that? Look, this is what Charlie ate.

Reveal the steak tin. Show them how it was done, then continue.

Why have I done this assembly just after talking about how racism or teasing someone because of their appearance is bad?

Take several answers. They should be able to work it out.

Yes, because when we are racist or call people rude names because of their appearance or what they wear, we are only looking at the outside. We are not thinking about the real person. We are not thinking about what they are like where it matters, on the inside.

You only looked at the outside of that tin. You didn't ask what was inside it.

I never said it was dog food, I said it was scrummy. It was, it was good, tasty steak/mince.

We must be careful that we don't make this kind of mistake with people. Just because someone looks different from us on the outside, that does not mean that they are different from us on the inside.

There is an expression that says you must not judge a book by its cover. Well you mustn't judge a person by the way they appear on the outside either.

Always find out what is on the inside of a person. If you don't, you could be missing a real treat.

Prayer

Dear Lord, you are the God of variety. You make so many different sorts of people. We are all beautifully and wonderfully made. You make each of us to be unique. Help us to appreciate the outside of each person and also to come to know the inside. You have taught us that what matters most is the inside of a person. Help us to learn this lesson.

Thought for the day

Let us appreciate the rich diversity of people in our school, knowing that what someone looks like on the outside is nowhere near as important as what they are like on the inside. Like the steak/mince, let us all try to be good and wholesome on the inside.

The raw potato smoothie

Theme

It is not only children who have difficulty in stopping themselves from saying inflammatory things. We all have moments when we have a choice between saying something that may cause trouble and not saying it.

This assembly is designed to give children a memorable visual image to help them to notice when they are about to say something that is going to cause trouble and then stop and consider the consequences.

Preparation

You will need:

- ✪ blender or a smoothie maker
- ✪ extension lead if no plug is available nearby
- ✪ box of fruit juice
- ✪ assortment of blendable fruit (e.g. 2 peeled oranges, 2 bananas, 1 peeled and cored pineapple cut into cubes, 2 peeled kiwi fruits, peeled and stoned mango, and any other suitable fruit left hanging about in school)
- ✪ washed raw, unpeeled, diced potato
- ✪ two or three mugs
- ✪ jug with water in it
- ✪ bucket
- ✪ slotted spoon.

The assembly

Good morning, everyone. Who likes smoothies?

So do I! I thought I would make a nice big jugful, then everyone who gets sent to me with good work this morning could have some.

Let's get on with it, shall we?

Make the smoothie as you talk. Do not use all the fruit. You will want some for the second smoothie you are going to make.

First, let's put in some fruit juice *[pour in a mugful]*. In that goes. Now let's put in a banana, and now some pineapple. In goes some mango and now some kiwi fruit. Now for some orange segments.

That seems about right. I'll plug in the blender. Now let's whizz it up.

Blend it all.

Well, that looks good. Now I'll taste it.

Oh, I don't like it! It's too sweet *[or thick or sharp or any other criticism you care to make]*.

Now pretend to lose your temper with your efforts.

Oh, that's it. I have ruined it. It's horrible. I am so cross. I don't want it any more. Right, I'm really fed up now. I'm going to put this potato in it, I don't care what happens. I'm fed up and cross. *[Throw in some diced raw potato.]*

[Still sounding cross and sulky.] If I press 'Go', this whole smoothie will be ruined. You can't eat raw potato. It is poisonous. But I don't care because I am cross and fed up.

Blend it.

Stop. Pretend to look horrified.

What have I done? Oh no! I have ruined the whole thing. I've ruined my smoothie. No one can eat it now. Why did I do that? Why did I put that potato

in? And why did I let my temper get the better of me? I didn't have to press the button. Right up to the last minute I could have taken the potato out.

I'll have to throw it all away.

You know, this is a bit like some of the arguments I hear in school.

One minute everything is going along very well. Children are playing in the playground or chatting while eating their lunch, and then suddenly a problem arises and someone responds by saying something unkind and ruins it all.

All sorts of unkind things get said in the temper tantrum that follows.

Children call each other by racist names, abuse each other's families and make nasty remarks about people's appearance. Sometimes they use really bad words and call each other 'thick' or 'stupid' or 'flid' or 'spacky'. Terrible things.

And once you have said them, it's too late.

It's like this smoothie here.

You can't get the potato out of the smoothie once you have pressed the button and you can't get the words back once you have said them.

What could I have done when I decided my smoothie was too thick/sharp/ sweet? *[whatever you said earlier]*.

Take suggestions – for example, you could have added sweeter fruit / added more juice / put in another banana.

Yes, you are right, I could have done any of those things.

What did I do that was silly? *[Take answers.]*

Yes, it was silly to lose my temper, silly to put potato in the blender and even sillier to press the 'Go' button.

When things go wrong in school we sometimes feel fed up and then we think of horrible things to say. That's like throwing the potato into the blender.

But then we say those horrible things. That's like pressing the 'Go' button.

I should have unplugged the blender and used this slotted spoon to fish out the bits of potato. Then I could have safely pressed the 'Go' button and made a scrummy smoothie.

It is just the same way when we are cross with each other. If we think of horrible things we want to say we should stop, take the unkind things out of the mix and say only sweet things and kind things. We should decide not to say the nasty things. Then we can press our own 'Go' button and start to speak.

You can't take the potato out of the smoothie once you have pressed the button and you can't take the unkind words out of the world once you have said them.

So let's learn to think before we press the 'Go' button and speak. Is what we say going to make a right potato smoothie of our friendships?

I can chuck this mess away, wash out the blender and make a new smoothie. You can't always do that with a friendship. It's best not to make the mess in the first place.

To end on an upbeat note, rinse out the blender jug and make a really nice smoothie with the fruit you reserved. Put it into the clean empty jug and dish it out as you said you would at the beginning.

Prayer

Dear Lord, sometimes we feel cross and angry with each other and we want to say really horrid things to each other. Help us to stop, think and not lose control of our tongues. Help us to take the unkind things out of the mix and say only the sweet things.

Thought for the day

Unkind words can make a real potato smoothie of our friendships.

A great help you are!

Theme

This assembly is about the whole idea of helping. Helping is a quite complex idea, especially with regard to helping others to help themselves.

This can also be a good introduction to understanding the concept of Fairtrade. We suggest you use it to start a Fairtrade project with the year-5 and year-6 children.

Preparation

You will need:

- ✪ king-size or double duvet cover
- ✪ four lengths of 10 cm (4 in) drainpipe – each piece should be the length of a child's arm from wrist to underarm; if this is too difficult to get, use four lengths of thick dowel
- ✪ roll of gaffer tape
- ✪ several wrapped sweets
- ✪ pair of scissors.

You will also need four children, whom you will select during the assembly:

- ✪ one must be very young or very small
- ✪ two may be any age (but not the sharpest knives in the box)
- ✪ one may be any age, any size, and of either sex – but they must have lace-up shoes.

The assembly

Good morning. Now, I need four volunteers.

Choose four children according to the above criteria. Bring them up to the front. Place them in a line, facing the school.

I am going to give each of you a task. You are all going to do your tasks at the same time and we shall see who is the winner.

Right, you first. *[To the small child.]* You have to fold up this duvet cover. You are to do it all on your own and it has to be so neat when you have finished that people would think it was new. *[Drop the duvet in front of the small child.]*

Now you two *[to the next two children]*, you have to have these sticks attached to your arms.

Attach the lengths of dowel to each of their arms with gaffer tape. This must make it impossible for them to bend their arms. Make sure you wrap the gaffer tape securely round their arms, like cuffs, every 15 cm (6 in) or so along their arms. Make sure the sticks cannot become detached.

You have to see how many sweets you can unwrap and eat in one minute.

Now move along to the last of the children, the one with the laced-up shoes.

Put your hands behind your back. *[Fasten their hands securely behind their back with a strip of gaffer tape. Then undo the laces in their shoes.]*

You have to do your laces up and run around the hall.

Now speak to the whole school.

I could do with a helping hand.

These four all have a task to do. *[Stand behind the little child with the duvet cover.]* This one has to fold up the duvet cover all on their own. I want this third *[indicate the left-hand side of the hall]* of the school to cheer for them.

These two have to eat as many sweets as possible, and you third *[indicate the middle third of the hall]* are to cheer for them.

And this one has to do up their shoe-laces and run around the hall. You lot *[Indicate the right-hand third of the hall]* are to cheer for her/him.

OK, you have one minute – go!

With luck, no one will have any success at all. The duvet is too big for the small child to fold, the sticks will prevent the pair of children from bending their arms, unwrapping the sweets and putting them in their mouths, and the gaffer tape will prevent the fourth child from doing up their shoe-laces. However, you are to encourage riotous cheering from the school. Let this continue for one minute.

Stop! How have you got on?

Well, no neatly folded duvet, no sweets eaten, and you are still standing there with your shoe-laces undone. Disaster!

But I am not surprised. The tasks were too hard. What did they need?

Take an answer.

Yes, they needed help.

Go over to the child with the duvet.

[Name] needed someone to help her/him. S/he is much too small to fold up this enormous duvet cover on her/his own.

Now go to the pair with the sticks.

What did they need to do? *[Take answers.]*

Yes, they needed to help each other. If they had fed each other the sweets, they could have eaten lots.

And what about *[name]*? What did s/he need?

Someone should say, 'S/he needed someone to do up her/his laces.'

Well, that would have helped in the short term. But what would happen when they came undone again?

What would be more helpful?

Hopefully someone will say, 'Cut the tape.'

Yes, s/he needed someone to cut the tape so that s/he could do up her/his shoes her/himself.

S/he needed someone to help her/him to help her/himself.

Give these volunteers a big clap.

Send them back to their places.

This is how help works.

Sometimes we need someone to help us. Life is too hard on our own.

Sometimes we need to help each other. It's not possible to do everything on our own.

And sometimes we need someone to help us so we can help ourselves. I think that last type of help is the most useful kind.

It is the reason why teachers teach you to read. They could read to you all the time, which would be helpful, but nothing like as helpful as teaching you to read for yourselves.

It is also the reason why we buy Fairtrade goods. We could send money to countries that are poorer than us, and that would be helpful, but not as helpful as our buying things directly from them at a fair price, and helping them to earn money from their businesses. When they can do that, they don't need charity any more.

If appropriate, tell the children that the year-5 and year-6 children are going to be thinking a good deal more about fair trade in the coming weeks.

So let's remember how we can be truly helpful people.

We can help someone who is having trouble, we can co-operate and help each other, and we can help others to help themselves.

Prayer

Dear Lord, you created love and you want us to care for each other. Help us to see when our love and help are needed and whisper into our heart what we should do. Let us care for each other in the ways you choose.

Thought for the day

Great opportunities to help others seldom come, but small ones surround us every day.

I'm not Jim and I can't always fix it

Theme

Recently we were watching a film that had a rather tense plot. One of the people we were watching the film with whispered, 'Is this film British or American?'

'British,' one of us replied.
'Oh dear,' she said, 'That means there might not be a happy ending.'
That made us think. What is an ending?

Most of our children are only at the beginning of their story, but already they may have had a good deal of difficulty to manage. As adults we want to help children and fix any problems they encounter. Sadly, we cannot always do that. We cannot ensure that each episode in the story of their lives always has a happy ending. We can't fix their parents' marriage difficulties, their dad's redundancy, their family's grotty house, their mum's alcoholism, their brother's aggression or their own learning difficulty. Yet we often want to. Children endlessly go to the adults in school with the request, 'Can you fix this?' We always try, but what should we do about the problems we can't fix?

Preparation

You will need:

❁ can of WD40 (you will not regret this purchase)

❁ wax crayon

❁ unwanted story book with a shiny cover

❁ permanent marker pen

❁ two items of no value made of plastic (e.g. a couple of broken toys)

- ✪ Tipp-Ex
- ✪ a few tissues or a soft cloth for cleaning
- ✪ chewing gum stuck on some fabric – an old school shirt, woollen jumper or socks from the lost property box would be ideal
- ✪ plastic bag containing a couple of ice cubes.

It is worth having a little practice before you do this assembly. The aim is to create some fairly usual scribbles and stains and then show the children how you can fix them.

We found that WD40 shifted crayon off walls, desks and book covers. It also removed Tipp-Ex from a desk and sticky-tape marks from walls.

Getting chewing gum off a shirt was much harder and our level of success was not great – but that serves the purpose of this assembly.

Collect all the items in the list above and place them on a table in front of the school. If you are using a Formica table you can probably scribble on this table – but practise first. Don't do anything irreparable to anything without testing it first in an invisible place, please.

The assembly

Good morning, everyone. Now, I was going to do a great deal of telling off this morning. You see, I have been going around school and I found all sorts of things I did not like.

I found crayon marks on desks, and I found sticky-tape marks on walls. I found a Tipp-Ex spill on a desk. I even found someone had scribbled with a permanent marker on a desk.

I was in a really bad mood. How could people be so silly as to ruin things in their own school? How could they be so careless as to break and damage so many things?

But then I found a book that told me how to fix almost anything. I hunted through this book and found some very helpful tips.

I need some volunteers.

Help your volunteers to use the WD40 to remove crayon from the shiny book cover, permanent marker from one plastic toy and Tipp-Ex from another. If you have any other miracle cleaning methods, now is the time to demonstrate them.

Congratulate the children on their success.

Ask another volunteer to come out and try to remove the chewing gum. You are supposed to freeze the chewing gum with the ice in the bag, then pick it off. I have never found this works terribly well. You can then ask if any one knows a better way.

Well, that wasn't too bad. We fixed a lot of things.

I also found out that this spray *[point to the WD40]* will remove stubborn temporary tattoos, felt-pen marks from the floor and the sticky stuff left on things after I have removed the price tags.

But, perhaps most usefully, you can spray it on trees to prevent beavers from chewing them. *[This is true.]*

Well, what can I say? So many problems fixed, and one or two *[point to the chewing gum]* not quite so successfully fixed.

This book was really good, so I looked up a few other things in it.

I looked to see if it could mend a broken heart or a broken friendship.
But there was nothing. That was too hard for this book.

Can you think how we can mend a broken friendship?

Take suggestions.

Those are definitely good ideas, but what would be better?

Would it be better if we had never broken the friendship?

How can we try to prevent broken friendships? *[Take answers.]*

Sometimes we can fix things, but it is not easy and it would have been a great deal better if we had been more careful in the first place and not broken them.

It would have been better if no one had scribbled on the walls or the books.

It would have been better if someone had put the lid on the Tipp-Ex.

It would be better if people were more careful with their friendships.

But sometimes things are broken and we can't fix them. Sometimes these are things that matter a great deal to us.

We can't fix our parents' marriage, and it's not our fault if it breaks.
We can't fix it when people are ill.
We can't always fix other people in our class.
We can't always fix other people's bad tempers.

Sometimes we have to accept that we can't always fix things. Not every episode in our life's story is going to have a happy ending. What can we do?

There are some things we can do.

If we see someone throw a plate on to the floor in a temper, we can't fix the smashed plate and maybe we can't fix their temper. But we can see that we need to learn not to behave like that ourselves.

In other words, we can learn from things.

Sometimes all we can do is to try our best to learn how to break as little as possible – to learn how to break as few hearts, as few plates and as few friendships as we possibly can in our life.

We learn a great deal from our assemblies, including today how to prevent a beaver from chewing our trees, but perhaps the most important thing we learn is this:

We can't fix others, but we can go a long way towards learning how to make the kind of choices that mean not so much gets broken around us.

Prayer

Dear Lord, we all have so many problems and difficulties. Sometimes we can see no way to sort them out.

You may like to use this well-known prayer instead: 'God grant us the serenity to accept the things we cannot change, the courage to change the things we can, and the wisdom to know the difference.'

Thought for the day

Sometimes we find we can't mend other people's lives, but we can always try never to damage them.

Training from Stay Cool in School

Margaret Goldthorpe runs an INSET training company called Stay Cool in School. This company helps schools to develop a clear ethos and promote self-discipline in learning and behaviour.

Training day topics include:

- a whole-school approach to encouraging self-discipline
- dealing with difficult people, including difficult parents

Parents' evenings

Stay Cool in School runs parents' evenings that are informative and entertaining, and are designed to help parents support their child's school in its management of their children's learning and behaviour.

For further information, please go to www.margaretgoldthorpe.co.uk

Margaret Goldthorpe
Stay Cool in School
Midsummer Cottage
Moor Lane
Sarratt
Hertfordshire
WD3 6BY

01923 262586
maggiegoldthorpe@gmail.com